AWS

Amazon Web Services. The Ultimate Guide for
Beginners, Intermediates and Expert.

By

Phillip Broyles

CONTENTS

INTRODUCTION

Amazon Web Services (AWS) is unquestionably one of the leading cloud computing services in today's industry. You may be pardoned if you're puzzled about how Amazon, which started as an online bookshop, has become the top provider of cloud computing.

Amazon Web Services (AWS) provides on-demand computer resources and services in the cloud, including billing pay-as-you-go. You will operate a server on AWS, for example, that you can sign in, install, stable, and run just as you would a computer that is right in front of you.

The entire concept draws upon the theory of cloud computing. This offers the IT network and other internet services.

AWS offers building blocks, which you can easily install to meet your workload. For AWS, you'll find a complete range of highly available tools built to work together to build apps that are scalable.

To delve into AWS you need to grasp their own terms and definitions. There is really a whole universe of cloud computing waiting for you.

Many mobile space developers are often unaware of the influence of the viral cloud and AWS in particular. We end up spending months writing software and server-side code for widely used features such as user registration, user login, password recovery, server-side data storage — services that are already supported by AWS and can be implemented within a fraction of the time. Amazon continues to threaten the existing technology provider group in its history, releasing new offerings and cutting prices at an unrelenting rate.

Whether you're looking for computing power, database storage, content delivery, AWS offers features to help you build advanced applications with greater flexibility, scalability, and reliability. AWS are engineered for most demanding requirements. It span beyond several global networks around the world.

In the next decade, AWS will be one of the highest ranked two or three global technology suppliers, and some of today's giants will be past tense, driven out of business, or forced into mergers due to their inability to meet and compete on Amazon's terms.

But in most cases (there's always a yet, isn't there?) getting started is always a problem that many people face while considering using AWS. But remains the worlds most robust and widely accepted cloud computing platform till date. Amazon Web Services documentation is pretty thorough, but you're not going to find a general guide for beginners to start from scratch and develop new skills.

CHAPTER ONE: GETTING STARTED WITH AMAZON

Are you thinking about how to get started on web services from Amazon? Have you seen a blockbuster on Netflix, bought a gadget from Amazon.com? You have used Amazon Web Services (AWS) in the past because they all use Amazon Web Services for their business, Netflix, Amazon.com. Amazon Web Services is the cloud computing market's largest platform.

Analysts claimed that AWS has more than 30 percent market share. Another impressive number: for the quarter ending in June 2017, AWS reported net sales of $4.1 billion. AWS data centers are also recognized worldwide, including in North America, South America, Europe, Asia, and Australia. But technology is invariably part of any cloud platform, making the difference for you as a customer who wants to provide a satisfying experience to consumers of your services.

Amazon Web Services as a Term

Amazon Web Services (AWS) is known to be a platform of web services that provide solutions for computing, networking, and storing under different patterns of abstraction. For instance, using block-level storage(an abstraction with low level)or a highly distributed object storage(an abstraction of high level) to keep your data. Websites can be hosted by using these services, run enterprise applications, and mine tremendous loads of data usage. Typical web protocols(such as HTTP)enable web services to be accessible via the internet, and this is practicable by humans or by machines through a UI. The most noticeable services provided by AWS are EC2, which offers virtual machines, and Simple storage system (s3), which offers storage capacity. Services provided by AWS work well together: they are useful for replicating your existing local setup, or you can probably design a new and fresh setup from scratch. The pricing model for the services is pay-per-use.

A customer of AWS, you can choose among different data centers. There is a worldwide distribution of AWS data centers. Take for sample, you might choose to start a virtual machine in London in the same manner as you would start one in Japan. This will help you to serve customers worldwide with a global infrastructure. In more general terms, AWS can also be called a cloud computing platform.

What Is Cloud Computing?

Invariably almost all IT solution is labeled with the term cloud computing or just cloud nowadays. Buzzwords like this may enhance profits, but they're most times difficult to work within a book. So for clarity, defining cloud computing will be helpful.

Therefore, Cloud computing, or the cloud, is referred to as a metaphor for the supply and consumption of Information and Technology resources. The information and Technology resources in the cloud aren't directly visible to the user; due to the presence of abstraction layers in between. The abstraction level offered by the cloud is in variation, which ranges from offering virtual machines (VMs) to providing (saas) software being a service based on complex distribution patterns. Resources are available on-demand in enormous quantities, and you pay for what you use.

Uses of Amazon Web Services

All sorts of applications can be run on AWS by making use of one or several combinations of web services. The illustrations given below will give you an insight of what you can do.

Hosting a Web Shop

John works as a CIO is an average-sized e-commerce business. He is interested in developing a supreme fast and convenient web shop. His first decision was to host the web shop on-premises, and three years earlier, he rented machines in a data center where a web server handles requests from customers, and a database stores product information and orders.

John did not only want to lift-and-shift his current on-premises infrastructure to Amazon Web Service, but he is interested to get the most out of this of the numerous advantages the cloud is offering. Additional Amazon Web Service permits John to step up his setup.

• Dynamic contents (such as products and their prices) and static contents (such as company logo) are contained in the web services. Getting these split would reduce the workload on web servers and enhance the performance delivery of static content over a content delivery network.

• Changing to maintenance-free services, which includes a database, an object store and also a DNS system, would allow john to be free of managing these parts of the system which, will decrease operational cost and improve its standard. Virtual machines permits the installation of the application running web shop.

Running a Java EE Application in Your Private Network

Mabel serves as a global corporation's senior system architect. When the data center contract expires within a few months, she wants to transfer parts of the business applications of her company to AWS, to reduce costs and gain flexibility. She wants to run business applications (such as Java EE applications) that consist of a server and an application and an AWS SQL database. She describes a virtual network for this purpose in the cloud and connects it to the corporate network through a Virtual Private Network (VPN) connection. Java EE application was run after installing an application server on a virtual machine. Mabel also wants to save data in an SQL database service (such as Oracle Database Enterprise Edition or Microsoft SQL Server EE).

For security, Mabel uses subnets to differentiate systems with different levels of security from each other.

If she makes use of access-control lists, she can determine the incoming and outgoing traffic for each subnet. For instance, in a scenario whereby the database is only accessible from the JEE server's subnet which helps to protect data that are of the critical mission. Mabel determines traffic to the internet by using (NAT) Network Address Translation and firewall rules as well.

Mabel has managed to connect the local data center with a virtual private network running remotely on Amazon Web Service to enable clients to access the JEE server.

To get started, Mabel uses a Virtual Private Network connection between the local data center and Amazon Web Service, but she is contemplating on bringing up a dedicated network connection to reduce the cost of network and increase network throughput in the future.

This turned out to be a huge success for Mabel.

She was able to limit the time needed to start up an enterprise application from months to hours, as Amazon Web Services can be used on virtual machines, databases, and even the networking infrastructure when needed within a few minutes.

Mabel's project also took advantage from costs of lower infrastructure on Amazon Web Services, compared to using their infrastructure on-computer.

Implementing a Highly Available System

Alex happens to be a software engineer for a rapidly growing startup firm. He is aware that murphy's law applies to IT infrastructure: and if anything goes wrong it is bad for the business. Alexa desire is to build a highly convenient and available system to prevent outages that might start running. Moreover. All services present on AWS are always either highly available or can be used in a highly available way. So, Alexa developed a system with a high architecture availability. The database service is offered with duplicate and fail over options. If the master database fails for instance, the standby database is promoted as the new master database automatically at no cost. Alex makes use of virtual machines acting as web servers. These virtual machines aren't highly available by auto, but Alex launches several virtual machines in different data centers to achieve high availability.

How Can You Take Advantage by Using AWS

It might occur to you that the most important advantage of using AWS is cost savings, but savings isn't the only benefit. We would see some other benefits of AWS. AWS announces new features, services, and growth as the day passes. AWS provides innovative technologies that help to generate valuable solutions for your customers and also helps to achieve a competitive advantage. Net sales of 4.1 billion USD was reported for the quarter ending in June 2017. That's a year-over-year growth rate of 42% (Q3 2016 versus Q3 2017). It is normal to expect AWS to expand the size and extend its platform in the upcoming years, for instance, by coming up with additional services and data centers.

Services Offers Solution to Common Problems

AWS is a platform that offers web services. Therefore, it solves the problem, which includes queuing, Sending mail, and storing files by services.

You don't necessarily need to repeat the wheel. All you are required to do is to pick the right services to build complex systems. So let AWS handle those services while you emphasize focus on your customers.

IT Enables Automation

It allows one write code to build networks, launch virtual machine clusters, transfer a logical database, because of the relationship between AWS and API. It improves efficiency, and reliability increases.

It becomes more difficult as the machine becomes more reliant on computer, the ability to work with graphs of any scale whereas a human being can easily lose focus. The Emphasis should be a focus on human activities being good and effective at, such as explaining a system and how to solve a program should be system development dependencies.

It Has Flexible Capacity (Scalability)

It transfer a logical database, because of the relationship between AWS allows one write code to build networks, launch virtual machine clusters and API. It improves efficiency, and reliability increases.

It Is Built for Failure (Reliability)

Many AWS services are fault tolerant or highly available by design. If these tools are used, you'll get flexibility for free. AWS lets you develop systems efficiently. It helps provide all that is needed to create your own highly available or fault-tolerant device.

It Reduces Time to Market

When a new virtual machine requests for the virtual machine boots in AWS and ready to use a couple of minutes later.it refers to any other available AWS service. It is used on-demand With shorter feedback loops, your development process can be eliminated faster constraint, such as the number of available test environments. It can be created in a few hours if the test environment is needed.

It Benefits from Economies of Scale

AWS is constantly increasing the global infrastructure, AWS benefits from an economy of scale. You will partially benefit as a customer from these effects.

AWS shrinks costs for its cloud services every now and then. Just a few examples: In November 2016, AWS reduces data storage charges for object storage S3 by 16% to 28%. AWS lowered the prices of virtual machines with a one-or three-year commitment by 10% to 17% in May 2017 — In July 2017, AWS lowered the prices of virtual machines running a Microsoft SQL Server (Standard Edition) by up to 52%.

It Aids Global Infrastructure

Do you serve customers all over the world? Using the global infrastructure of AWS has the following advantages: low network latencies between your customers and your infrastructure, being able to meet regional data protection requirements, and taking advantage of different infrastructure prices in various regions. AWS provides data centers in North America, South America, Europe, Asia, and Australia so with little extra effort you can deploy your applications worldwide.

They Are Professional Partners

When using AWS services, you can be confident that the new requirements and certifications are met for their quality and safety. ISO 27001 — a worldwide information security standard certified by an independent, accredited certification body, for example:

- ISO 9001 — a standardized approach to quality management used worldwide and certified by an independent certification body.

- PCI DSS Level 1— A Payment Card Industry (PCI) (DSS)Data Security Standard to protect data from cardholders.

The Cost of Amazon Web Services

An AWS bill is like an electric bill. Services are charged on the basis of use. You bill for the amount of time a virtual machine was operating, the object store storage used, or the number of load balancers running. Services are to be invoiced monthly.

The pricing for each service is available to the public; AWS Simple Monthly Calculator can be used when you want to calculate the monthly cost of a planned setup.

Free Tier

Within the first 12 months of signing up, you can use some AWS services free of charge. The idea behind the Free Tier is to allow you to experiment with AWS and use its services to gain some experience.

Here's a taste of what's included in the Free Tier: a small virtual machine running Linux or Windows for about 750 hours (about a month).

This means that for a whole month you can run a virtual machine or you can run 750 virtual machines for an hour. Classic or application load balancer 750 hours (or roughly a month).

- Object store with storage of 5 GB.

- Limited 20 GB storage space, including backup.

When you reach the Free Tier cap, you will start paying without further notice for the services you use. Upon the end of the month, a bill will be received. Before you start using AWS we will show you how to monitor your costs. You bill for all the services you use after your one-year trial period is over. But there are certain services that are safe for ever. For starters, NoSQL's first 25 GB database is free for ever.

Billing Example

As mentioned earlier, you can be paid in several ways: — a virtual machine is charged per minute based on minutes or hours of use. A balance of loads is charged per hour.

- Traffic-based — Traffic is measured, for example, by gigabytes or by number of requests.

- Depending on storage use — Use can be determined by capacity (e.g. 50 GB volume, no matter how much you use it) or by actual use (e.g. 2.3 GB).

Suppose your web shop began successfully in January, and you've run a marketing campaign to increase sales for the next month. Lucky you: in February you have been able to increase the number of visitors to your web shop five fold. As you already know, use-based payment for AWS is required.

Pay-Per-Use Opportunities

New opportunities are provided through the AWS pay-per-use pricing model. The obstacle to starting a new project, for example, is removed, as you no longer need to spend front-end in infrastructure. Upon launch, you can start virtual machines and pay only per second of use, and you can stop using those virtual machines whenever you want and no longer pay for them. You need not to make an initial decision about how much room you are going to use. Another example: a large server with the same capacity costs exactly as much as two smaller ones. So you can split your systems into smaller components, because the cost is the same. This makes tolerance of failure affordable not only to large investments but its also applicable to smaller budgets.

Alternative Comparison

AWS is not the only source of cloud computing. The major players also includes Google Cloud Platform (GCP) and Microsoft Azure and the Google Cloud Platform (GCP). Much in common are the three big cloud providers. We all have: A global infrastructure that offers facilities for computing, networking, and storage. An IaaS service delivering on-demand virtual machines: Amazon EC2, Azure Virtual Machines, Google Compute Engine. Highly distributed storage and I / O power scale-free storage systems: Amazon S3, Azure Blob storage, Google Cloud Storage.

A pricing model pay-as-you-go. But what are the cloud provider differences? AWS is the market leader in cloud computing, providing a broad product portfolio. While AWS has grown in the business sector in recent years, it is still clear that AWS has begun with services to solve problems on the internet. Ultimately, AWS builds great services focused on innovative technologies, often open source. AWS offers complicated, yet rock-solid ways to restrict your cloud infrastructure access.

Microsoft Azure offers the technology stack in the cloud for Microsoft, which has recently expanded to include web-centric and open source technologies. It would seem that Microsoft is making a lot of effort to catch up with Amazon's market share in cloud computing.

GCP focuses on developers seeking sophisticated distributed systems to be developed. Google combines its global infrastructure to provide scalable and tolerant services (such as Google Cloud Load Balancing). In our view, the GCP is more focused on cloud-native applications than on migrating the local-hosted applications into the cloud. There are no shortcuts to make an informed choice about which cloud provider to pick. Every case for use and each project is different. In the details is the Devil. Don't forget where you're from, too. (Do you use Microsoft technology heavily? Do you have a large team of system administrators, or are you a developer-centric company?) Ultimately, in my opinion, AWS is the most mature and powerful cloud platform currently available.

Exploring Amazon Web Services

Hardware for storing, networking and computing, is the foundation of the AWS cloud. AWS runs services on this hardware. The API acts as an interface between your applications and AWS services.

You can manage services by sending requests to the API manually via a web-based UI like the Management Console, a command-line interface (CLI), or programmatically via an SDK. Virtual machines have a special feature: you can connect to virtual machines through SSH, for example, and gain administrator access. This means you can install any software you like on a virtual machine. Other services, like the NoSQL database service, offer their features through an API and hide everything that's going on behind the scenes.

Users send HTTP requests to a virtual machine. This virtual machine is runs a web server along with a custom PHP web application. The web application needs to talk to AWS services in order to answer HTTP requests from users. For example, the application might need to query data from a NoSQL database, store static files, and send email. Communication between the web application and AWS services is handled by the API.

The number of services available can be scary at the outset. When logging into AWS's web interface you are presented with an overview listing 98 services. On top of that, new services are announced constantly during the year and at the big conference in Las Vegas, AWS re: Invent. AWS offers services in the following categories:

- Analytics

- Desktop and App Streaming

- Media Services

- Application Integration

- Developer Tools

- Migration

- AR and VR

- Game Development

- Mobile Services

- Business Productivity

- Internet of Things

- Networking and Content Delivery

- Computer

- Machine Learning

- Security, Identity, and Compliance

- Customer Engagement

- Management Tools

- Storage

- Database

Unfortunately, it is not possible to cover all services offered by AWS in our book.

Interacting with Amazon Web Services

You make calls to the API that communicates with the API when you interact with AWS to configure or use services: the Management

Console, the Command-line inter. The API is the entry point for AWS, here is an overview of the available face tools, the SDKs and the blueprint for the infrastructure. We are going to compare the various tools.

Management Console

The AWS Management Console helps you to control and navigate AWS resources via a graphical user interface (GUI) that runs on every modern web browser (the current three versions of Google Chrome and Mozilla Firefox; Apple Safari: 7, 8, and 9; Windows Internet Explorer: 11; Microsoft Edge: 12). The Management Console is the best place to start, when you start or experiment with AWS. This helps you gain a quick overview of the various services. The Management Console is also an excellent way to develop and test a cloud infrastructure.

Command-line Interface

The command-line interface (CLI) allows you to manage AWS services within your terminal and to access them. Because you can use your terminal to automate or semi-automate recurring tasks, CLI is a valuable tool. The terminal can be used to create new cloud infrastructures based on blueprints, upload files to the object store, or get the details of your infrastructure's networking configuration regularly.

If you want to automate some pieces of your infrastructure with the help of a continuous integration server, like Jenkins, the CLI is the right tool for the job. The CLI provides an easy way to access the API and combine multiple calls into one script. Even by chaining multiple CLI calls together you can start automating your infrastructure with scripts. The CLI is available for Windows, Mac, and Linux, and there is also a PowerShell version available.

SDKs

Interact with the AWS API using your preferred programming language. AWS offers SDKs for the following platforms and languages:

- Android

- .NET

- Ruby

- Browsers (JavaScript)

- Node.js (JavaScript)

- iOS

- PHP

- C++

- Java

- Python

Usually, SDKs are used to incorporate AWS services in applications. If you are designing apps and want to incorporate an AWS application such as a NoSQL database or a push-notification program, the right choice for the job is an SDK. Some services need to be used with an SDK, such as queues and topics.

Blueprints

A blueprint is a summary of your program that includes all of its resources and dependencies. An Infrastructure as Code tool compares your blueprint to the current system, and calculates the steps to create, update, or delete your cloud infrastructure. If you have to monitor many or complex environments, consider using the blueprints. Blueprints can help you make your network setup in the cloud automated. For example,these can be use to set up a network and start virtual machines. You can also automate your infrastructure by writing your own source code with the help of the CLI or the SDKs. But doing so requires that you resolve dependencies, ensure that you are able to update different versions of your infrastructure and handle errors on your own.

CREATING AN AMAZON WEB SERVICES ACCOUNT

Firstly,what you need to do is create a very own AWS account. You sign up for the service in this multistep process, provide your billing information and then verify your agreement with AWS to create your account.

1. Show your favorite web browser at http:/aws.amazon.com to the main Amazon Web Services page.

2. Click the button to Sign Up.

Technically, if you have one, you can also use your existing Amazon retail account, though I don't advise. Think about it— if you share your AWS account and use a retail ID for it, someone you're sharing your AWS with may end up buying a nice large flatscreen TV on your dime down the line. And my advice is that you create a new account with AWS.

3. Make sure the I Am a New User radio button is selected, fill in a suitable e-mail address in the given field and then press the Sign In Using Our Secure Server button.

4. Enter a username, your e-mail address (two times, just to be sure), and your password (again, twice, just to be sure).

5. Click the button Continue.

Doing so brings up the Account Information screen, requesting information about your address and phone number. You are asked to select the box that confirms you agree with the terms of the AWS customer agreement.

6. Enter the appropriate personal information, confirm your customer agreement acceptance and then click on the Create Account and Continue button.

The next page asks you for a credit card number and the information regarding your billing address. Amazon wants to get paid for sure, right?

7. In the appropriate fields enter the required payment information, and then click Continue.

The next page you see is a little strange-looking. Amazon wants to confirm your identity, so they are asking for a phone number that they can use to call you.

8. Type your telephone number in the correct field and press the Call Me Now button.

On the screen, AWS shows a pin code and then calls you to the phone number you received.

9. Answer the phone and enter on the telephone keypad the displayed PIN code.

10. Click the button to Continue.

You're asked to wait a little for AWS to start up your account, but in my experience it's not more than two or three minutes. You will then receive an e-mail confirming your account setup; to complete the account signup process, you need to click on a link in that e-mail. After setup, you should see a screen that lists all the services you've already signed up for automatically, simply by creating your account. Quite a striking list, eh?

Two important points to exclude from this initial account setup are as follows:

1. Your account is now built as an AWS general account. You can use AWS services anywhere in the AWS system— the US East or either of the two western US territories, Asia Pacific (Tokyo, Singapore, or Australia), South America (Brazil), and Europe (Ireland). Simply put, your account is scoped over AWS as a whole, but resources are within a specific region.

2. You have given your credit card number to AWS to pay for the resources you are using. In turn, with AWS, you have an open tab, so be careful how much computing power you consume. You don't have to worry much about costs for the purposes of this book— your initial sign-up provides a free level of service for one year that should be sufficient for you to perform the steps in this book as well as experiment yourself without breaking your piggy bank.

SIGNING IN TO YOUR AMAZON WEB SERVICE

You now have an AWS account and are willing to join the AWS Management Console.

The Management Console, as mentioned earlier, is a web-based tool that you can use to control AWS resources; it makes most of the AWS API functionality available to you. Enter your email address, click Next, then enter the password you want to sign in. The navigation bar at the top is the most important part. It consists of seven sections:

1. AWS— Management Console start page, including a summary of all services.

2. Services — Gives fast access to all AWS services.

3. Resource Groups — Provides an overview of all of your AWS resources.

4. Custom section (Edit)—Click here to personalize the navigation bar with the edit icon and drag-and-drop important services.

5. Your name— Let you access your account and billing information, and let you sign out, too.

6. Your Region — let your region be chosen. You need not change anything right now in here

7. Support — Gives you access to forums, documentation and a ticket system Next, you will open a key pair to connect to your virtual machines.

You will then build a main pair to connect to your virtual machines.

CREATING A PAIR KEY

A key pair is a private key, and a public key. The public key is inserted into the virtual machine and uploaded to AWS. Your private key is; it's like your password but it's much more secure. Protect your private key, as though it was a password. It's your secret, so do not lose it— you can't get it back.

You use the SSH protocol to access a Linux machine; during login, you will use a key pair to authenticate instead of a password. When making use of Remote Desktop Protocol (RDP) to access a Windows machine, you'll need a key pair to decrypt the administrator password before you can sign in.

The following steps will guide you to the EC2 service dashboard offering virtual machines and where a key pair can be obtained:

1. Open the AWS Management Console at https:/console.aws.amazon.com.

2. Click Navigation bar Services, and select EC2.

3. The EC2 Dashboard should now be activated by your browser.

Follow the steps below to create a new key pair:

1. Click Key Pairs in the Network & Security navigation bar.

2. Click button Create Pair Key.

3. Call mykey Key Set. If you choose a different name, the name must be replaced in all the following examples throughout the entire book!

You download a file named mykey.pem during the key pair creation process. Now you need to plan the key for potential use. You need to do things differently depending on your operating system so please read the section that suits your OS.

Create a Billing Alarm to Keep Track of Your AWS Bill

At first, AWS ' pay-per-use pricing model might feel unfamiliar to you, as what your bill will look like at the end of the month is not 100 percent predictable. The Free Tier covers most of the examples in this book, so AWS won't charge you anything. There are clearly marked exceptions. To give you the peace of mind you need in a comfortable environment to learn about AWS, you will create a billing alarm next. If your monthly AWS bill exceeds $5 USD, the billing alarm will notify you via email so you can react quickly.

Naturally the first step is to open the AWS Management Console on https:/console.aws.amazon.com.

1. In the top of the main navigation bar, press your Name.

2. From the pop-up menu, click My Billing Dashboard.

3. Go to Settings using the left-hand sub-navigation.

4. Select the check box for Receiving Billing Alerts.

5. Click Preferences Save.

You can create a billing alarm now. Here are the steps to do this:

1. On https:/console.aws.amazon.com, open the AWS management www.

2. In the navigation bar, open the Services and select Cloud Watch.

3. Click the link to generate an alarm billing.

Enter the threshold for the Billing Alarm for total monthly charges. We propose as threshold $5 UDS, the equivalent of the price for a cup of coffee. In case your AWS bill exceeds the threshold, type in the email address where you want to receive notifications from your billing alarm. To create your Billing Alarm, click Create Alarm.

Over the inbox. An email from AWS appears that contains a link to confirmation. To complete your billing alarm setup, click the Confirmation button.

That is the whole thing. If your monthly AWS bill for any reason exceeds $5 USD, you'll be notified immediately, enabling you to react before unwanted costs occur.

CHAPTER TWO: INTRODUCING THE AWS API

The AWS ecosystem functions as an integrated set of hardware and software services designed to allow simple, efficient, and cost-effective use of computing resources. Essentially an API is a way of communicating with a computing device. As far as AWS is concerned, nothing is done without using the AWS API. The AWS API is the only way external users interact with AWS resources and there is literally no way to use AWS resources without involving the API. Yes, if you use the AWS Management Console or the command line tools to access AWS, you are simply using tools that make calls to the AWS API.

APIs: Knowing the Basics You through think of yourself as the kind of person who would never have to use an API. You would be incorrect. APIs were important, they're important now, and they're going to become even more important. More often than not, you used APIs for years without even thinking about them. The API is the only public interface for computing resources and services with respect to Amazon. Nothing is done without making API calls. As I stated earlier, the API is short for the application programming interface.

A fair way to describe an API is to say it represents a way for one program to connect with another through a given interface— that is, a mechanism through which any other program that interacts with the program can be assured that it will fulfill its purpose. The idea is that if a calling program provides the correct information in the correct syntax, the program will respond in the manner requested by the API.

Understanding APIs

Traditionally, the term API referred to the programming interface offered by one or more routines which was bundled into a function library. Someone would provide a library that, say, performs date-and-time manipulation functions. A software engineer would bundle that library into a program and then call those functions through the API offered by the library. The API represents the "contract" offered by the library. The API defines the functional interface, the format of any information provided to the functions (commonly referred to as arguments or parameters) within the library, the operation to be performed and the output each function would return to the calling program.

One advantage of this "contractual" approach is that it provides encapsulation inside the library — the actual code enforcing the contract is shielded from the calling function. The library code can then be modified, updated, or even completely replaced with another set of code, all without disturbing the calling function— as long as the new library code complies with the old contract.

Encapsulation allows for much more versatility in software environments, since different parts of the overall environment are developing at different rates; modifying one aspect of the system doesn't require change. As long as the contract is adhered to, any other portion of the environment can remain unchanged. The definition of the term API has been extended: Instead of being used exclusively to describe libraries that are directly connected to other programs, it is now used to refer to software environments where the various software programs operate on different servers and interact across a network. In addition, that network can be contained within a single data center or, quite commonly, be extended over the Internet. This network-based approach to the API is often referred to as an infrastructure for web services — remember how Amazon's cloud computing platform is called Web Services? That is not an accident.

The whole notion of security is one critical factor that web services require, but not traditional API libraries do. If two programs communicate over the Internet, the one calling the service must be able to provide information about who it is (its identity), and the service called must be able to validate that whoever makes the call is permitted (authorized) to access the service requested.

An Overview of the AWS API

The only way to interact with the AWS is through its API. Any service you may ever use is called (and returns data) via its API, so it is critical to use the API to work with AWS. But don't worry about having to know the details of a low-level programming interface— you'll probably never have to interact with the API directly. Nevertheless, you need to at least understand the broad outline of how the AWS API works.

The AWS API Delivery (Soaps or Rest)

You can choose how to offer Web services from a couple of different schools of thought. The older approach, SOAP (short for Simple Object Access Protocol), had broad support from the industry, complete with an extensive set of standards. Unfortunately, those standards were too comprehensive. The people who design SOAP built it to be highly flexible— it can communicate through the web, e-mail and private networks.SOAP were also defined to ensure security and manageability with A number of supporting standards.

SOAP is based on a document encoding standard known as Extensible Markup Language (XML, in short), and the SOAP service is defined in such a way that users can then leverage XML regardless of what the underlying communication network is. However, the data transferred by SOAP (commonly called the payload) also needs to be in XML format for this system to work.

31

Do you notice a pattern here? The drive to be comprehensive and versatile (or to be all things for everyone) plus the necessity of XML payload meant that SOAP ended up being quite complicated, making it a lot of work to use properly. Many IT people, as you might guess, found SOAP daunting and hence resisted using it.

A doctoral student defined another approach to web services as part of his thesis around a decade ago: REST, or Representational State Transfer.

(Frankly, I think he first coined the term REST, because it sounded easier and more relaxing than SOAP, and then configured the name to fit the acronym.) REST, which is far less comprehensive than SOAP, aims to solve fewer problems. It doesn't address some aspects of SOAP that seemed important but that made it more complex to use in retrospect— safety, for instance.

The most important aspect of REST is that it is designed to integrate with standard web protocols, so that standard web verbs and URLs can be used to call REST services. A legitimate REST request, for example, would look like this: http:/search.examplecompany.com/CompanyDirectory/Employee Info?Empname= BernardGolden

That's all it takes to ask the example company's REST service to see my personal details. The HTTP verb that accompanies this request is GET, requesting the return of the information.

You use the verb DELETE to delete information. You use the verb POST to insert my details.

You use the verb PUT for updating my information.

Additional information would accompany the empname for the POST and PUT actions, and would be separated by an ampersand (&) to indicate another argument that the service would use.

REST does not impose specific formatting requirements on the service payloads; it differs from SOAP, which requires XML in this respect. For simple interactions, a string of bytes is all you need for the payload; the JSON encoding convention is used for more complex interactions (say, besides returning my employee information, I want to place a request for the employee information of all employees whose names begin with G). (JSON, if you're curious, stands for Javascript Object Notation.) As you might expect, REST's simpler model of use, its alignment with standard web protocols and verbs, and its less restrictive payload formatting made it catch up with developers like a house on fire.

AWS originally launched interactions with its API with SOAP support, but it has steadily deprecated (reduced its support for, in other words) its SOAP interface in favor of REST. My recommendation that you focus on using REST for any use of the AWS API is. So, you won't end up with systems that stop working one day— long after you've forgotten the specifics of the processes of interaction. Unfortunately, I have experienced— many times— the unpleasant task of having to go back into a system and try to reconstruct my actions from months or years before. Tempting fate with AWS doesn't make sense— if you want to connect with the AWS API, use REST, which is the long-term direction Amazon provides.

The AWS API As you might expect, the AWS API is one huge puppy, considering the comprehensiveness of AWS services and the way Amazon has been developing and expanding them.

However, if you take a quick look at the following example of an API call, it closely resembles the (quite simple) REST example: https:/ec2.amazonaws.com/?Action= RunInstances & ImageId= ami-60a54009 & MaxCount=3 & MinCount=1 & Placement. AvailabilityZone= us-east-1b & Monitoring. Enabled= true & AUTHPARAMS

AWS is instructed to run between one and three instances based on an ami-60a54009 Amazon machine image and place it in the us-east-1b availability zone. AWS provides monitoring capabilities and AWS is instructed by this call to allow this monitoring. The AUTHPARAMS component is a stand-in to the information that AWS uses in its API to enforce encryption.

AWS API Security

Here's an factual question when handling third-party proxies: If these tools act on your behalf, how does AWS know that you are in fact the person on whose behalf they act? In other words, how can AWS authenticate your identity to make sure that you get the commands it receives? The same question actually holds true even if you interact directly with the AWS API. How can AWS validate your identity so it can only execute commands for you?

Of course, one option is for you to use your account username and password in calls to the API.

Although some cloud providers are taking the path, Amazon isn't.

Instead of depending on a username and password, two other keys are used to authenticate the API service calls: the authentication key and the hidden access key. It uses these keys to implement security in service calls in a way that is far more secure than using only your username and password.

How does that work, then? Once you sign up with AWS for an account, you will be able to create an access key and have a hidden access key sent to you.

Each one is a long string of random characters, and the longer of the two is the secret access key.

You should store it somewhere very secure when you download the secret access key, because it is the key to implementing secure service calls. After that, you and Amazon both have a copy of the access key and the secret access key. Keeping a copy of the secret access key is important because it is used to encrypt information sent back and forth between you and AWS, and if you don't have the Secret Access Key, you can not execute any service calls on AWS. The way the two keys are used is conceptually simple, albeit in detail a little challenging.

Essentially, you (or a tool operating on your behalf) do the following for every service call you want to carry out:

1. Create payload for calling service

These are the data to send to the AWS. It may be an object that you want to store in S3, or an image identifier that you want to start.

(You'll also attach other pieces of information to the payload, but I don't list them here because they vary according to the specifics of the service call. One piece of data is the current time)

2. Use secret access key to encrypt the payload

Doing so ensures no one can examine the payload and find out what's inside it.

3. Sign the encrypted payload digitally by adding the secret access key to the encrypted payload, and using the secret access key to perform a digital signature process.

Secret access keys are longer and more random than typical user passwords; the lengthy secret access key makes the encryption performed with it more secure than it would be if a typical user password were used.

4. Send the total encrypted payload, together with your access key, via a service call to AWS.

Amazon uses the access key to look up your secret access key for decryption of the payload. If the decrypted payload represents readable text that can be executed, then the service call is executed by AWS. Alternatively, it assumes that something is wrong with the call to service (maybe it was called by a malevolent actor) and does not perform the call for service.

In addition to the encryption that has just been described, AWS has two other methods used to ensure the legitimacy of the call to service:

1. The first is based on the date information included with the service call payload, which it uses to determine whether the time associated with making the service call is appropriate; if the date in the service call is significantly different from what it should be (in other words, much earlier or later than the current time), AWS concludes that it is not a legitimate service call and discards it.

2. The second additional security measure shall include a checksum for the payload calculated by you. (A checksum is a number representing the content of a message.) AWS calculates a checksum for the payload; if its checksum does not agree with yours, it disallows and does not execute a service call. This approach to checksum ensures that no one tampers with a message's content and prevents a malevolent actor from intercepting a legitimate service call and changing it into an inacceptable action. If somebody tampers with the message while AWS calculates a checksum, the checksum will no longer suit the one included in the message, and AWS will fail to execute the call.

If you are using a proxy system to communicate with AWS— the AWS management console, a language library, or a third-party application— like most AWS users, you need to provide the proxy with your activation key and hidden access key. When executing AWS service calls on your behalf, the proxy includes the access key in the call, and uses the secret access key to encrypt payload.

Because these keys fulfill a critical role in AWS, you should share them only with entities that you trust. If you want to try out a new third-party tool and you don't know much about the service, set up an AWS test account for the trial rather than using your AWS account credentials for the development. Therefore, if you decide not to go forward with the product, you can drop it, terminate the AWS test account and move on, unconcerned about potential security vulnerabilities in your main manufacturing system. You can of course always create new access keys and secret access keys, but using your production keys for testing and then changing the keys creates a lot of work, because you need to update every location that makes reference to your existing keys. If you're like many other AWS users, you'll be using a number of tools and libraries to update your keys, and going back to them is a pain. You're better off testing new tools using nonproduction accounts.

AWS offers a service which facilitates the management of keys / secret access keys. It's termed IAM.

IAM allows you to delegate keys and hidden access keys to individuals or programs, making it much easier to prevent wholesale changes when one person leaves an organization; it is also of great help when you need to give access to the AWS services and resources that you need for each application.

CHAPTER THREE: SETTING UP AMAZON WEB SERVICE STORAGE

Every journey has got a start. I strongly recommend that you take a long, hard look at storage to start your journey through AWS, for several reasons:

1. Storage is an increasingly important issue for IT, owing to the recent dramatic rise in data used by companies in their day-to-day operations. While traditional structured data (the database) is growing quite rapidly, businesses are exploding with the use of digital media (video). IT organizations are increasingly using storage, and often look to communications service providers (CSPs) like Amazon for storage. Another storage demand factor is the recent rise of big data, which is about processing very large datasets. Companies are drowning in data and many find it almost impossible to keep up with the management of their own storage systems on-site.

2. Storage is Amazon's first offering on the AWS. Storage, therefore, holds an important place in the AWS ecosystem, including some extremely innovative uses over the years by AWS customers of its storage services.

3. Several AWS offers rely on AWS storage, notably Simple Storage Service (S3). Understanding AWS storage services help you understand better the operation of the AWS storage offerings.

4. AWS is continuing to innovate, delivering new storage services. For example, Glacier provides a fresh twist when dealing with a historic IT issue: archival storage.

The term storage service from Amazon (which may be the largest in the industry) is a misnomer: within AWS, the company provides four different storage services. The scale of the overall storage service that subsumes all four particular services is huge. Simple Storage Service (known as S3); S3 has grown so rapidly in just over six years that it now contains more than two trillion objects. To put S3's staggering growth into perspective, the service spent six years reaching 1 trillion objects and growing from 1 to 2 trillion objects in less than ten months.

1. Simple Storage Service (S3): Provides highly scalable object storage in the form of unstructured collections of bits.

2. Elastic Block Storage (EBS): Provides highly available and reliable data volumes that can be attached to a virtual machine (VM), detached, and then reattached to another VM.

3. Glacier: A data archiving solution; provides low-cost, highly robust archival data storage and retrieval

4. DynamoDB: Key-value storage; provides highly scalable, high-performance storage based on tables indexed by data values referred to as keys.

Differentiating the Amazon Storage Options

Simply put, the huge growth in storage makes traditional approaches (local storage, network-attached storage, storage-area networks, and the like) no longer suitable, for these three reasons:

1. Scaling: Traditional methods simply can not scale up large enough to handle the volume of data that companies now generate. The amounts of data that businesses need to manage, outstrip nearly all capabilities of storage solutions.

2. Speed: We are unable to move data rapidly enough to satisfy the demands businesses put on their storage solutions. To be frank, most corporate networks can not manage the level of traffic needed rather shunt around all of the bits held by the businesses.

3. Cost: In view of the volumes of data being addressed, the solutions established are not economically viable— they are not affordable at the scale that businesses now require.

For these reasons, the problem of storage has long moved beyond local storage (for example, disk drives inside the server using the data).

Over the past few decades two other types of conventional storage have entered the market— network-attached storage (NAS) and storage-area (SAN) networks— that transfer data from the local server to the server-attached network. Instead of looking for a local disk, it seeks it over the network when the server needs data.

The two types of network-based storage differ materially (though their acronyms are similar). NAS, which acts as an extension of the server's local file system, is used as local files: Reads and writes the same work as if the file was stored on the server itself. To put it another way, the NAS lets data appear as part of the local server. SANs do work very differently.

They offer separate remote storage from local server; that storage does not appear as local to server. Instead, the server must operate a special protocol to communicate with the SAN device; you can say that the SAN device provides detached storage that the server needs to make special arrangements for use.

Both types of storage continue to be widely used but the much larger volumes of data make it impossible to support requirements for either NAS or SAN storage.

As a result, newer types of storage have come to the fore which provide better functionality.

In particular, there are now two new types of storage: 1. Object: Retrieves and stores unstructured digital objects reliably 2. Key-value: Manages structured data Object storage Object storage provides the ability to store, well, objects— essentially digital bits collections. These bits may represent a digital photograph, an MRI scan, a structured document such as an XML file— or the video of the embarrassing attempt your cousin made to ride a skateboard down the steps in the public library (the one you premiered at his wedding).

Object storage provides efficient (and highly scalable) storage of bits sets, but does not enforce structure on the bits. The structure is chosen by the user, for example, who needs to know whether an object is a photo (which can be edited), or an MRI scan (which requires a special application to view it). The user will know both the object's structure and methods of manipulating it. The object storage service simply ensures that the bits are stored reliably.

Storage of objects differs from storage of files which you may be more familiar with using a PC. File storage offers functionality for updating, and storing objects does not. Suppose you are, for example, storing log output from a program. The program constantly adds new logging entries as events happen; it would be incredibly inconvenient to create a new object each time an additional log record is created. By contrast, using file storage allows you to update the file continuously by adding new information to it— in other words, updating the file as the program creates new log records.

The storage of objects offers no such capability for updating. You can insert an object, or retrieve it, but you cannot change it. Instead, in the local application, you update the object, and then insert the object into the store. To allow the new version to retain the same name as the old version, delete the original object before inserting the same name on the new object. The difference may seem minor but different approaches are needed to manage stored objects.

Distributed key-value storage unlike object storage, distributed key-value storage provides structured storage that is somewhat similar to a database but differing in important ways to provide additional scalability and performance.

Maybe you've already used a relational database management system— a storage tool commonly known as RDBMS. Its data rows have one or more keys (hence the key-value-storage name) which support data manipulation. While RDBMS systems are fantastically useful, scaling beyond a single server is usually challenging to them. From the get-go, new distributed key-value storage products are designed to support huge amounts of data by spreading over multiple (maybe thousands of) servers.

Key value storage systems often make use of hardware resource redundancy to prevent outages; this concept is important when running thousands of servers because they are bound to suffer hardware breakdowns.

Without redundancy, a single server can knock the entire storage system out of commission; using redundancy always makes the key-value system available— and, more importantly, your data is always available because it is protected against hardware outages.

There are literally dozens of storage products that are of key value. Many of these were first developed by so-called web-scale companies, such as Facebook and LinkedIn, to ensure they could handle massive traffic volumes. Those companies then turned around and released the products under open source licenses, so you can use them in other environments now (or anyone else). While key-value storage systems vary in different ways, they do have these common features:

1. Data is structured with a single key to identify the record that contains all remaining data. The key is almost always unique — for example a user number, a unique username (for example, title 1795456), or a part number. This ensures that each record has a unique key which makes it easier to scale and perform.

2. Retrieval is for the key value only. For example, every record has to be checked to find all records with a common address (where the address is not the key).

3. There is no support for conducting searches for common data elements across multiple datasets. RDBMS systems allow joins: Find all records in a second dataset that have the username in individual records for a given username in a data set. For example, in order to find all books that a library patron has checked out, perform a user table join (where the user's last name is used to define their library ID) and the book checkout table (where each book is identified along with the library IDs of everybody who checked out). To execute this query, you can use the join functionality of an RDBMS system; by contrast, because key-value

systems do not support joins, the two tables would have to be matched at the application level rather than the storage systems. Using this concept, commonly described as "the intelligence resides in the application," executing joins requires "smarts" application and lots of extra coding.

Key-value storage is a trade-off between usability and scalability, and trade-off is skewed towards scalability (and less user-friendliness).

The abundance of storage forms provides consumers with a much richer set of options for handling data associated with their devices. While they gain much more flexibility and can adapt the storage solution to functional requirements, they do face a challenge: to handle a larger number of storage solutions, a broader set of skills is required. It also requires them to manage hundreds or thousands of servers using a key-value solution.

Luckily, Amazon recognizes that all of these storage solutions are important, even with the management challenges they bring with them and offers four storage solutions. A user can select one that is appropriate to their needs— rather than being forced to shoehorn a solution into their application that does not support the functionality required.

The need for flexibility in storage is why Amazon offers four storage types.

You may not need all four-with just one or two, many users manage. You should understand all the options offered by AWS, because then you may choose to pursue a new option rather than rely on the existing one.

Storing objects in the Simple Storage Service (S3) Bucket Simple Storage Service (fondly called S3) is one of the best, most versatile and, of course, most commonly used AWS offerings. Calling S3 "the filing cabinet of the Internet" is no exaggeration. Its object storage is used by individuals and businesses in a huge variety of applications, such as:

1.Dropbox: This file storage and syncing service uses S3 to store all the documents it stores on behalf of its users.

2. Netflix: This popular online video-consumer service uses S3 to store videos before moving to its content delivery network. In fact, Netflix operates nearly 100 per cent on AWS, making it a little bit like a poster child for the service.

3. MEd commons: In S3, this company stores health records of customers online— and, by the way, it complies with the strict requirements of the Health Insurance Portability and Accountability Act (HIPAA).

Hundreds of large and small businesses (and individuals) use S3 to store information used within their enterprises.

S3's richness and versatility are restricted by the imagination alone. The variety of ways it's being used is mind-boggling. And Amazon continually upgrades S3, adding features to make it even more useful.

S3 has evolved into a highly functional storage service which is widely used. How wide-spread? Cedexis, a company that analyzed a large sample of enterprise applications, found that S3 had been accessed by 25 per cent. The reason for this is simple: S3 is so useful, so easy to use and so cheap that it infiltrates applications almost seductively.

S3 Storage Basics

Let's get down to the brass tacks and explore how S3 works. S3 objects are treated as web objects— that is, a URL identifier is used to access them via Internet protocols. In this format every S3 object has a unique URL:http:/s3.amazonaws.com/bucket/key. An actual S3 object using this format looks like this: http:/s3-us-west-1.amazonaws.com / aws4dummies / Cat+ Photo. JPG

Now, you might ask what the bucket and key are, listed in the first example?

Within AWS, a bucket is a set of objects. The name of the bucket is associated with an account-for example, my aws4dummies account is associated with the bucket called aws4dummies. The name of the bucket needn't be the same as the name of the account; it can be anything. The bucket namespace is completely flat though: Each bucket name must be unique among all AWS users. If you try to create a test bucket name within your account, you will see an error message, as you can bet your bottom dollar that someone else has claimed that name already. (So you know, the account is limited to 100 buckets.)

Bucket names have a number of restrictions, as described in;

http:/docs.amazonwebservices.com/AmazonS3/latest/dev/BucketRes
trictions.html

My recommendation: keep simple names easily understood, simplify the use of S3 and avoid problems.

A key in AWS is an object's name, and it serves as an identifier for finding the key-related data. In AWS, a key can either be an object name (like in Cat+Photo. JPG) or a more complex arrangement that imposes some structure on object organization within a bucket (like in bucketname / photos / catphotos / Cat+Photo. JPG, where /photos / catphotos are part of the object name). This simple arrangement includes a common directory-like or URL-like format for entity names; however, it does not represent the actual S3 storage system structure— it is simply a convenient and recognizable way of naming objects, making it easy for people to keep track. While many applications view S3 storage as if it were in a common file folder structure (including the AWS Management Console itself), they do not say anything about how objects are stored in S3.

Control of objects S3 An object S3 is not a complex creature— it is simply a collection of bytes. The service does not impose any restrictions on the format of the object-it is up to you. The only limitation is on object size: 5 TB is limited to an object S3. (That's big.) Managing S3 objects as with all AWS offers, S3 is accessed via an application programming interface, or API, and supports both SOAP and REST interfaces.

You probably won't, of course, use the (not really user-friendly) API to post (create), get (retrieve) or remove objects from S3. You can access them via a programming library that encapsulates the calls to the API and offers easier-to-use, higher-level S3 functions. However, more likely you will be using an even higher-level tool or application that provides a graphical interface for managing S3 objects. However, you can be certain that calls to the S3 API are somewhere down in the depths of the library or higher-level tool. In addition to the most obvious and useful actions for objects (such as post, get, and delete), S3 offers a wide range of object management actions— for example, an API call to get the object's version number.

S3 works around this problem by allowing the versioning of S3 objects — you can, for example, modify version 2 of an S3 object and store the modified version as version 3. This involves updating objects outlined earlier: retrieving old object, modifying object in application, deleting old object from S3, and then inserting modified object with the original name of the object.

S3 Bucket and Object Security

AWS offers fine-grained access controls to implement S3 security: You can use these controls to explicitly control who-can-do-what with your S3objects. The mechanism by which this access control is enforced is, naturally enough, the Access Control List (ACL). These four types of people can access S3 objects:

1. Owner: The person who created the object; he can also read or delete the object.

2. Specific users or groups: Particular users, or groups of users, within AWS. (Access may be restricted to other members of the owner's company.)

3. Authenticated users: People who have accounts within AWS and have been successfully authenticated.

4. Everyone: Anyone on the Internet (as you may expect). S3 provides a rich set of actions in the S3 API. Several functions, for example, allow the manipulation of object versions to retrieve a certain version of an object. And, of course, I mention elsewhere the expiration capability that was added early in 2012 — it's in the API as well. The access controls specify who, and the actions specify what — who has the right to do what with a given object. The interaction between the S3 access controls and the object actions gives S3 its fine-grained object management functionality.

S3 USES, Large and Small

It is difficult to make specific recommendations on what to do with S3, because it is extremely flexible and capable. Individual (and not corporate) users tend to use S3 as a stable, location-independent digital media storage system. Another typical personal use for S3 is to back up local data, either through the AWS management console or through one of the many consumer-oriented backup services.

Companies are using S3 for the same reasons as individuals, and use cases for many more. For example, businesses store content files that their partners use in S3. Many consumer electronics and appliance manufacturers now sell digital format user manuals; others store those files in S3.

Most businesses put images and videos that are used in their corporate websites in S3, reducing their problems in storage management — and ensuring that website efficiency is not hampered by insufficient network capacity under heavy web traffic conditions.

Interestingly enough, the most common S3 activities revolve around making, removing, and deleting items.

Here is the common lifecycle of an S3 object: create the object in preparation for its use; set permissions to control access to the object; allow applications and individuals to retrieve the object as part of the functionality of an application; and delete the object when it is no longer required by the application that uses the object. Of course, as they are evergreen, many artifacts are never removed: they have a long-term function.

As you become more familiar with S3, you will no doubt start exploring additional S3 features. S3 includes encryption of objects stored in the database, protecting the data from anyone attempting unauthorized access to them. When objects are accessed, and by whom, you can log requests made against S3 objects to audit. S3 can even be used to host static websites: they do not dynamically compile data to create the website-served pages — eliminating the need to run a web server.

Many of the electronic computing tools you use (or will use) as part of your personal or business life make use of S3; it is widely used as one of the solutions provided by both large and small technology companies.

S3 Scope and Availability

S3 accessibility, and how you use it to access objects, is just one piece of the puzzle; you also need to understand S3's overall structure.

AWS as a whole is organized into regions, each with one or more accessibility zones, or AZs. Although S3 locates buckets within regions, keep in mind that the names of S3 buckets are unique across all regions of the S3, although buckets themselves reside in specific regions. For example, if you build a bucket named after your business, you need to choose which region the bucket will be placed in.

In the cat photo example I mentioned earlier in this chapter http:/s3-us-west-1.amazonaws.com / aws4dummies / Cat+ Photo. JPG you see that the aws4dummies bucket is located in the western region of the US. (Note the URL section s3-us-west-1.) All objects in the aws4dummies bucket have to reside in the US West. No big deal, Okay?

Okay, it does rely on that. When an AWS virtual machine (VM) has to access an S3 object and the VM and the object are located in the same AWS area, Amazon does not charge the network traffic carrying the object from S3 to EC2. Nevertheless, if the VM and the item are in different regions (traffic is transported over the Internet), AWS can charge a few cents per gigabyte— which can be expensive for very large objects or heavy use.

One way around this problem is to locate multiple buckets in each region with duplicate objects and tweak the names of the buckets to avoid conflicts— for example, by renaming my aws4dummies to aws4dummies us west and creating similarly named buckets in all other regions. I can then build duplicate objects in each of the similarly named buckets to remove network traffic charges anywhere I run an EC2 instance (although with much greater complexity and somewhat higher charges to save all duplicate items).

S3 Example

The nuts-and-bolts of how to install and upload and launch an S3 bin. (If you want to see how it's going to happen, go over there.) In this segment, I'm going through a standard action that would happen after you've got an AWS account and built an S3 bucket. You are likely to use S3 from apps, of course, so I'll show you an example of the S3 API. If you want to attach an entity, the API call will look similar to this example.

```
PUT /my-image.jpg HTTP/1.1

Host: myBucket.s3.amazonaws.com

Date: Wed, 12 Oct 2009 17:50:00 GMT

Authorization:                                              AWS
AKIAIOSFODNN7EXAMPLE:xQE0diMbLRepdf3YB+

FIEXAMPLE=

Content-Type: text/plain

Content-Length: 11434

Expect: 100-continue

[11434 bytes of object data]
```

Of course, you may want a higher-level abstraction within your code. AWS provides SDKs for several languages, including PHP. To perform the same insert operation in PHP, follow this example:

```
require_once 'sdk.class.php';

$s3 = new AmazonS3();

$bucket = "*** Provide bucket name ***";

$keyname1 = "*** Provide object key ***";

$filepath = "*** Provide file name to upload ***";

$response = $s3->create_object(
```

$bucket,

$keyname1,

array'fileUpload' => $filepath,'contentType' => 'text/plain',)

These actions are common to the two examples of code:

1. Provide credentials for approving actions: in the line starting with Authorization, you can see this directly in the API request. You placed the access key and hidden access key in environment variables that the SDK can retrieve when assembling the call of the API on your behalf.

2. Defines the action: This is the line starting with PUT in the API; in the PHP SDK it is the call to create object.

3. Bucket Identification: This stage determines where the object should be placed.

In the call of the API the bucket is marked as myBucket in the host.s3.amazonaws.com. It's $bucket in the PHP example, which would be loaded with the name of the bucket.

4. Identify the name of the object key: This index describes the object inside the container. It's my-image.jpg in the API; it's $keyname1 in the PHP example, which would have been set to the index name you selected at the top of the example file.

5.Identify the object: it is the "item" that must be stored in the bucket S3. The example of an API has a placeholder marked with[11434 bytes of object data].

The actual bytes which compose the object would have followed in a real-life API call. The code points to a file to upload in the PHP example, and the path to it is stored in $filepath.

6. Identify the type of content: This determines the type of data AWS manages in the bucket and uses a suitable program to manage any interaction with the file. (Be aware that my examples use test / plain here.)

S3 Cost

S3 has a simple cost structure: You pay for each gigabyte of storage your objects use. You are also paid for calls to S3 from the API which do not differ by number.

Finally, you are paying for the network traffic that comes from delivering S3 items.

Storage costs for the first terabyte start at $.095 per gigabyte per month, and they move downward as total storage rises to $.055 per gigabyte per month for more than 5000 terabytes of demand.

The cost of using the API varies from $.01 per 1,000 requests (for PUT, COPY, POST, or LIST calls) to $.01 per 10,000 requests (for GET and any other request).

DELETE applications are free of charge.

Pricing for data transfer— for transfers into or out of an AWS area— varies by volume (as you can suppose). Transferring data into is a privilege— there is no fee for inbound network traffic that positions data in S3 storage. There's no fee on the first gigabyte of traffic for outbound traffic. Then the price is $.12 per gigabyte up to 10 TB, with scale-based pricing lowered.

The price of traffic between 150 TB and 500 TB is reduced to $.05 per gigabyte.

Also, Amazon offers reduced redundancy for S3 storage, which keeps fewer copies of your data — and trades cost-reliability. Reduced redundancy storage starts at $.076 per gigabyte of storage and decreases at volumes higher than 5,000 TB to $.037 per gigabyte.

Managing Volumes of Information with Elastic Block Storage (EBS)

The Elastic Block Storage (EBS) is volume-based storage that is not associated with any particular instance; rather, additional storage is connected to instances. Another way of saying this is that an EBS volume is unique, and has a different lifetime from EC2 instances. For this instance, it can be attached to any instance to provide storage, but is detached when it terminates from the instance. (If you've ever interacted with SAN storage, you're familiar with the concept. If you haven't operated with SAN storage, don't worry — EBS is easy to understand.) However, you'll almost certainly work with EBS, because it's extremely useful and solves several significant limitations in AWS.

The EBS storage service operating on the network is distributed in volumes, which can be connected to an EC2 instance and used just like a disk drive. Since a volume may become unformatted, it needs to have a (formatted) file system installed on it before it can be used. For example, if you want to add an EBS volume to a Linux machine, first you need to format the volume in one of the many Linux file system formats and then mount it to the instance file system, which enables the operating system to access the volume of EBS and read and write to the volume.

Because an EBS volume is network-based it can last longer than any particular instance. Thus, an EBS volume provides persistent storage that is safe from loss when an instance is terminated or crashes. The most common (although definitely not only) use case for EBS is the database server filesystem. The storage of the database is put on the volume of the EBS, which must be connected to an instance running the database software so that the software can read and write to the storage of the EBS database.

This process is a bit more complicated than using the storage of the instance itself, but it has a great virtue: By using EBS, the application owner can ensure that data is not subject to loss caused by interruption of instances. Even if the instance crashes the volume of the EBS is free from loss of data. A new instance can be created, the volume of the EBS can be added to it and the instance can start operations in the database again.

The consumer can set the size of an EBS volume and can range from 1 GB to 1 TB. Volumes are connected to accounts and are by default restricted to 20 per account.

EBS Reliability

EBS can make your applications more reliable, since the storage is separate from any particular instance (as mentioned in the previous section). Your data stays nice and safe, no matter what happens in an instance.

How confident is EBS itself, though? Why protect yourself against instance failure, after all, if the EBS service itself is unreliable?

Amazon has again used redundancy with EBS to boost reliability. Although Amazon discloses few details about its service, it states that multiple copies of each volume of EBS are available to protect against data loss from hardware failure at all times. If a disk drive containing an EBS volume goes wrong, Amazon must make a new drive available and copy the EBS volume data to the new drive to ensure adequate backup stays on.

Although EBS is highly reliable, AWS has endured several major outages, and the culprit has turned out to be EBS at least a few times. What's it up to?

The storage aspects of the EBS service are not to blame. Instead, the management layer of EBS (or control plane, a geeky term meaning...

EBS management layer) has failed. The control plane is part of the intelligent software for the AWS infrastructure and unfortunately, problems may arise.

Not to minimize the problems associated with the outages but try to see them as the inevitable by-products of the innovation represented by AWS.

(EBS has been around only since 2008 and, believe it or not, AWS is only a few years older.) Failure inevitably occurs in any new and different product. Compare AWS reliability to that of your own data center if you are concerned about outages. Normally, this analogy helps to put AWS outages into context and explains them as less troubling.

EBS SCOPE AWS as a whole is organized into regions with one or more accessibility zones (AZs) in each. With EBS, volumes within a given region reside in a single AZ. When you create an EBS volume, you define which AZ should (only) be located within a given region. These statements, of course, imply that any instance of EC2 that needs to mount and use this volume of EBS must be located within the same AZ.

A setup like this clearly presents a challenge. While Amazon maintains multiple copies of the volume of EBS, they are all located inside the same AZ.

So does this not conflict with the general advice for making applications more robust by allowing them to operate in (or be able to operate in) multiple AZs, or even across AWS regions?

The short reply is yes. If your application uses volumes of EBS (and, frankly, most do), following AWS best practices and operating your applications across multiple AZs will be more difficult. Luckily, there is a relatively straightforward way to tackle this issue— using EBS snapshots. (I inform you more about that later in this chapter— for now, take it for granted that the constraint that EBS volumes live in a single AZ is not insurmountable.) Using EBS To use EBS, simply build the volume using the AWS API or (more likely) using either the AWS Management Console or a third-party device. As mentioned earlier in this chapter, you must attach it to a suitable operating system device on a running EC2 instance before you can start using the volume, and then format it with a file system that is appropriate for the operating system. Afterward, the volume is ready for use. As part of your preparation work, it is already attached to a running EC2 instance and you can start using it immediately.

You simply detach the volume when you decide to terminate the EC2 instance to which you have attached the volume (again, via the AWS API or Management Console, or a third-party tool that you are using). The volume of the EBS moves into a quiescent state, ready to attach to a new instance of the EC2 whenever you choose. Actually, it's even easier than that— when you terminate an EC2 instance, AWS detaches the volume for you, although best practices suggest not relying on the automatic detachment.

Many people completely avoid the manual attachment / detachment effort and instead implement an automated approach by configuring the launch process of the EC2 AMI to automate the EBS attachment process. (AMI refers to Amazon Machine Image, which is the format EC2 stores instances in which they are not running actively.) Alternatively, many tools (Amazon or third parties) do this work and avoid the need to implement it within the AMI. These tools start an AMI and then execute commands for attaching the volume to the API.

EBS Performance

Obviously, if volumes of EBS are used for important application resources, such as databases, you might wonder if their performance is crucial. How do you rank them?

Typical EBS performance is around 100 IOPS (I / O operations per second) — for which EBS is intended. The question is, what is EBS's true-world performance?

Well, it does depend on that. (You may not like that answer, but it's true. Here's why.) As I noted in this chapter earlier, EBS is network-based storage: it's remote from the instance that's attached. All data reads and writes to the volume, therefore, must pass through the AWS network— and this is where things get tricky.

Any time data has to pass through a shared resource like a network, it's subject to delays and interruptions caused by other applications traffic. (This, by the way, is true of all data center environments, not just AWS.) The standard way to address this problem is to create a dedicated storage network (thus the term storage area network, or SAN).

Faithful to its roots as a low-cost company, Amazon did not implement a dedicated network for its EBS service, leading to the big EBS complaint— spotty performance. Overall, EBS output wasn't that great, but even worse, because of the question of network congestion induced by other applications, it appeared to be highly incoherent.

In mid-2012, AWS addressed this shortcoming by extending the EBS service with Provided IOPS for EBS — designed to deliver rapid, predictable EBS performance.

The IOPS supplied delivers guaranteed throughput to EBS volumes between 500 IOPS and 4000 IOPS. It requires the use of EBS-optimized instances, which, presumably via the use of a dedicated storage network, provide dedicated throughput. With Prevised IOPS volumes, the same volume striping strategy across multiple EBS volumes can be used to increase performance well beyond the 4000 Mbps limit.

In accordance with AWS pricing, there is an increased cost for Provided IOPS use, as I explain later, in the "EBS pricing" segment. It will be necessary to determine if the better, more reliable EBS output associated with Provided IOPS is acceptable and therefore worth paying for. Provided IOPS costs aren't that high, but you can always hold off for a while, and then move to Provided IOPS, if necessary.

EBS Snapshots

You may recall that volumes of EBS are always associated with a single Availability Zone (AZ) which can pose a challenge if a major goal is to create highly available applications. You may also remember that I suggested some way of working around the challenge. I'll let the other shoe go down here and tell you everything about the solution.

Aside from the persistent storage of EBS, AWS also offers another function within EBS: the snapshot. It is a point-in-time data backup that takes place within an EBS volume. In S3, the snapshot is stored in the same region where the volume of EBS resides.

Following the creation of an initial snapshot of an EBS volume, subsequent snapshots only store the modified volume bits. So if you have a volume of 10 GB, and you create an initial snapshot, all the volume data is in the snapshot.

Volume snapshots which are created later only store bits which have changed since the previous snapshot. An EBS snapshot is thus a highly efficient way of ensuring the durability of the EBS data, even if the EBS volume itself was to be lost or damaged in some way.

A snapshot can be used to create a new volume, so you create a new volume via a snapshot instead of starting with an empty volume, and when it is connected to a running case, all the data in the original volume is available to you.

EBS Pricing

EBS pricing follows the normal AWS method of charging for what you are using and is relatively straightforward, though you should consider the part of the equation that you are using. Keep in mind that new AWS accounts get a certain amount of EBS usage at no charge, making it easy to get started (and cheap!). Keep in mind also that you will encounter minor variations in the price of EBS depending on the region in which the volume of EBS resides. The variance is about 10 per cent, so keep it in mind when planning. The prices described in this section are reflective of the region of AWS USA East.

EBS storage costs $.10 a month per gigabyte. (By way of comparison, in the Singapore region, the fee is $11 per GB per month, which gives you a concrete example of regional volume location-related price variations.) AWS also charges EBS volume I / O requests— $0.10 per million I / O requests.

The IOPS that is supplied is a little trickier. For storage, you pay a slightly higher rate—$.0125 per gigabyte per month (in the U.S. Eastern region of AWS). You'll also pay $.10 per month of IOPS. The delivered IOPS can measure up to 4000 IOPS per volume. So if you're using a full month of 1000 Provided IOPS, you're paying $.10 times 1000, or $100.

A snapshot costs $0.095 a month per gigabyte. But it's not a straightforward calculation to understand exactly how much storage a volume snapshot will require. AWS compresses snapshots, so a 10 GB EBS volume snapshot does not fill up to 10 GB. In addition, subsequent volume store snapshots only copies of the blocks that have changed in volume since the previous snapshot was taken, further reducing the amount stored, and thus how much you pay for the subsequent snapshot. So the first Snapshot, 5 GB. When 10 percent (1 GB) of the volume is adjusted before the next snapshot of a 10 GB EBS volume will (with compression) take only, the snapshot would contain 1 GB (or less, in reality, as compression would be applied to this snapshot). As you can see, estimating the exact cost of using an EBS volume is not an easy matter to see. In contrast, it's cheap per gigabyte. For most organizations, the bigger issue comes up when they start using lots of AWS resources. Even though the cost of EBS per gigabyte isn't too expensive, if you use lots of resources, it can add up — especially if your staff create a bunch of volumes that aren't used. Whether it is in use or not, you pay for the room.

Managing Archive Material with the Glacier Storage Service Glacier, launched in August 2012, is a storage service based on a crucial (though often poorly managed) IT requirement: storage of archives.

Archival storage is simply stated to be backup data of any kind. Archival storage is best known for server backups— complete dumps of all data on the server drive. With the rise of NAS and SAN technology, of course, backups today also include storage device data dumps.

Glacier is designed to address the shortcomings of a number of traditional archive solutions, none of which, as you will soon find out, are completely satisfactory.

The tape archive is the oldest archive-storage solution. Data is written to a device that stores data on magnetic tapes, which are then sent off-site to ensure that no on-site disaster can wipe out all data, both live and archived, from a company. Those issues burden the archiving of tape: 1. It's expensive: Usually you have to use a commercial, off-site storage facility, and it costs a lot — businesses sometimes even trim the amount of data they archive. The approach is appealing but if it gets worse and the on premise data disappears it can become a big problem.

2.It's inconvenient: you need to transfer the tapes to the off-site storage location and, if you need to retrieve material from the archive, you need to return the tapes physically and extract them from the tap.

3. It's slow: Sending and receiving physical tapes is obviously slow because you need to move them. A secondary slowness factor-writing and reading tapes-is a very slow process. Removing data from tape will take hours (or even days, if your archive tapes are disorganized and you need to pick up the data you want through a variety of tapes) 4.It's insecure: your tapes are off-site. Somebody can get them and read the data from the tape, placing the security and privacy of your data at risk.

5. It may not work: Tape archives are infamous for failing to function properly, and the original data writing to the tape may ultimately deteriorate in storage.

CHAPTER FOUR: MAKING USE OF VIRTUAL MACHINE (ELASTIC COMPUTE CLOUD EC2)

A virtual machine is a part of a physical machine that is removed on the same physical machine by software from other virtual machines; it includes CPU, memory, network interface, and storage.

EC2 is one of the most innovative of AWS services because a fundamental part of IT has changed: the use of provisioning servers. EC2 delivers very fast virtual servers, all via self-service. Compared with how things used to be handled, it is hard to overestimate the change this approach stands for.

Typical applications for a virtual machine are as follows: Hosting a web application such as WordPress — Operating an enterprise application such as an ERP application — Transforming or analyzing data such as encoding video files Starting a virtual machine—

Launching a Virtual Machine

Starting a virtual machine takes only a few clicks:

1.   Open   the   AWS   management   console   at https:/console.aws.amazon.com.

2. Rest assured you're in the N. The region of Virginia (US East), as we have optimized our examples for this region.

3. Find, and click, the EC2 service in the Services navigation bar.

4. Click Start Instance to start a virtual machine Wizard.

Selecting the Operating System

Choosing an OS first step. In AWS, the OS for your virtual machine comes bundled with pre-installed software; this bundle is called an Amazon Machine Image (AMI). Choose Ubuntu Server 16.04 LTS (HVM) and Why Ubuntu?

Because Ubuntu offers a ready-to-install link checker package which you will use later to check for broken links on a website.

The AMI forms the basis from which your virtual machine begins. AMIs are available through AWS, third party providers, and the community. AWS provides the Amazon Linux AMI based on Red Hat Enterprise Linux and optimized for EC2 use. You will also find popular Linux distributions and AMIs with Microsoft Windows Server, and in the AWS Marketplace, you will find more AMIs with pre-installed third-party software.

Start by thinking about the application specifications you want to run on the VM when selecting an AMI. Another important factor in deciding which AMI to start with is your knowledge and experience with a specific operating system. You also need to trust the publisher of the

AMI. We prefer to work with Amazon Linux, as AWS manages and optimizes it.

Configuring Details, Storage, Firewall, and Tags

The wizard's next four steps are easy because you don't have to adjust the defaults. You can change the details for your VM, like network configuration or VN launch number. Leave the defaults for now, and then press Next: Add Space to start.

There are various options on AWS to store data, Keep the defaults and press Next: Add Tags. A clean house is indicative of a clean mind. Tags assist you with organizing resources on AWS. Each tag is nothing more than a pair of key values. Add at least one Name tag for this example to help you find your stuff later. Using Name as the base, and the value for my machine. Tap Next then: Configure Security Group.

A firewall helps keep your virtual machine safe.

1. Choose New Security Group Building.

2. Type the name and description of the security group in ssh-only.

3. Maintain the default rule which allows SSH from anywhere.

4. Click Check and Begin to continue with the next step

5.

Connecting to Your Virtual Machine

You can do remotely downloading additional software and executing commands on your virtual machine. To log in to the virtual machine, you'll need to find out its public domain name:

1. Click on the EC2 module in the Services navigation bar, and click Instances in the left submenu to switch to a virtual machine summary. Pick the virtual machine from the table by clicking

2. Click Connect to open the Virtual machine link instructions.

Seeing the Unique Nature OF EC2

EC2 is based on virtualization— the process of using software to create virtual machines which then perform all the tasks that you would associate with a "real" computer using a "real" operating system. If you have any virtualization experience you can recognize the framework of EC2.

The base, however, isn't all for everyone. There are significant differences between EC2 and conventional virtualization, typified by-products like VMware ESX and Citrix XenServer — differences you can easily notice when you start using EC2. A virtual machine is either running or quiet in a standard virtualization product (a fancy way of saying "not running"). EC2 has developed its own terminology: If a virtual machine runs in EC2, it is referred to as an instance; if an instance does not run in EC2, it is referred to as an image. Likewise, a virtual machine is started in virtualization, and an instance is launched in EC2.

Understanding Images

An image is a collection of bits required to create an instance running. This collection comprises the items described in this list:

1. The operating system that runs on the instance at least: this means that it can be Windows or Linux.

2. Any software packages you have chosen to install: the package may be a software you have written or a third-party provider package (assuming, of course, that the software license supports this kind of use). For example, together with the load balancer HAProxy, you can include the Apache web server— both are open source products that can be freely included in your image.

3. Any configuration information required for the instance to function properly: for example, in an image containing Ubuntu, Apache, and HAProxy, configuration information may be included for HAProxy to interact with the same instance Apache server. Adding this information to the image prevents any time you start the image from having to configure the packages.

4. Owned by me: images created by your account, whether you are the sole user of your account or share it with others; may include both private and public images.

5. Amazon images: Images created and made available by Amazon to anyone who wants to use them

6. Public images: images which are owned by other accounts but made available to anyone who wants to use them

7. Private images: Images you own and made available to you only or to other accounts you specify

8. EBS images: images used as storage for the AMI

9. Elastic Block Storage (EBS). Images from Instance-Store: Images stored in Simple Storage Service (S3) 10. 32-bit: images built on 32-bit operating systems (either instance or can be EBS-backed)

11. 64-bit: images built on 64-bit operating systems (either instance or can be EBS-backed)

12. AWS Marketplace: images created by third parties that are available at a fee.

EC2 Image Sizes

If you think the variety of instance types makes it difficult to decide what to do, the variety of image sizes will map the image. Suffice it to say that AWS provides a wide range of image sizes which should enable you to meet the performance needs of your application by tuning the EC2 infrastructure on which it runs.

The original type of instance (Standard) aims at a good mix of resources to meet the requirements of standard applications, well. The other instance types include a greater amount of one type of resource in terms of the instance's other resource types; one type of instance may then be better able to support a particular set of application specifications than another.

Your Petition

EC2 spectrum EC2 images and instances found within AWS regions which can pose a problem if you want to be able to run the instances in multiple areas. Why would you want your instances running in multiple regions now? I'm delighted to hear you ask:

1. As protection against failure in an AWS availability zone (AZ) or region: If AWS has suffered an outage in one portion of its service area, you can continue to operate your application in another available area or region.

2. To minimize latency when serving users located in specific geographic areas: by putting instances in, say, the Asia Pacific region based in Australia, you can reduce overall network transit time to neighboring users.

3. To ensure the best possible results for a user base spread around the world, you can run a multi-regional application: in addition to the need to handle photos at multiple locations, you can take advantage of two additional AWS services: Route 53: Amazon's centralized CloudFront DNS service: Amazon's S3-based content delivery network

4. To comply with national data privacy requirements: some countries

impose restrictions on the locations where their citizens or business-related data resides. You may choose to run your application in multiple regions to meet these.

EC2 pricing and deployment options restrictions In addition to the various types and sizes of EC2 offerings, EC2 offers three deployment options. To put it another way, the same form and size instance will pay a different hourly rate, depending on how you choose to deliver it. Each choice to deploy influences pricing:

1. On-demand: When you choose, you launch certain instances. Here, for every hour they run, you pay the standard rate.

2. Reserved: In these instances, you pay an upfront fee and receive a reduced rate in return for every hour they run. There are some variations of reserved deployment options which I will discuss in this chapter later.

3. Spot: For these instances, you offer a bid price— a price you're willing to pay for every hour that they run. Amazon runs a reverse auction for spare EC2 capacity and runs every spot instance for which bids that meet or exceed the "clearing" price of the spot instance have been   received.

CHAPTER FIVE: NETWORKING

In the AWS scheme of things, networking is a big deal. Without it, there would be no sending and receiving network traffic from any of the AWS instances.

In networking, however, as in all other pieces of AWS design, Amazon came up with solution that is clearly ingenious— but just as clearly different from the traditional solutions that most people are familiar with. And for the same reasons, it broke ground in other facets of its design: increasing size and promoting automation, AWS took the path less traveled.

We do so over a network as machines speak to each other. This talking activity takes place on a TCP / IP network for the purpose of computing done around the globe. The standard of the TCP / IP network utilizes the concept of layers to illustrate how communication takes place. The layers are numbered 1, 2, and 3, in this model:

1. The physical layer (Layer 1): is associated with the cables that sit in your office, or how your wireless access point speaks to your computer's wireless card.

2. The data-link layer (Layer 2): controls the data flow between network entities (hosts, domain names, subnet, whatever) that reside on

the same network; this local area network (LAN) is dedicated to a single organization.

Usually, these organizations have a network interface card (NIC), each of which has a unique identifier— their Media Access Control (MAC) address. Layer 2 sets out how two entities that have MAC addresses can send data to each other.

3. The network layer (Layer 3): controls the flow of data between network entities residing on different networks. (Note that this data is sent via NIC, a convenient piece of hardware that is stored on a server.) Users communicate across multiple LANS in this wide-area network (WAN) and can't count on being connected on the same local physical layer. Layer 3 most often works by using the Internet Protocol (IP) to communicate using a logical addressing scheme (so-called, logically enough, IP addresses). IP addresses most commonly have four digits — say, 10.1.2.3 — with eight-bit data sets representing each digit.

Digital LANS

Keeping data private In a virtual networking environment (and do not forget that this is precisely what a cloud computing service provides at its core), how can you guarantee one user that their data is not available to another user? Obviously, one way is to create separate physical networks and allow each user account to have its own local area network, but that would be a logistical (and extremely expensive) nightmare. In addition, this method would require each user to have their own router to communicate all of their Layer 3 traffic to other, outside users.

Routers have been upgraded to provide specific users with Virtual LANs (VLANs) that essentially cordon off sections of larger, shared networks. Within that VLAN, traffic flows through Layer 2; any traffic flows through Layer 3 to other parts of the shared network, or out over the Internet.

Most hosting companies use VLAN technology to assign each customer a VLAN so that their computers are segregated from the computers of other customers.

This strategy, which provides the customers with a secure networking solution, tells them that their network traffic is immune from interception.

In general, during account setup, most hosting companies do all the work related to manually assigning and configuring VLANs. A network administrator will access the provider's router and configure the new customer's VLAN. The computers of the customer are then placed on the newly configured VLAN, and network traffic flows over it to them.

As hosting companies have moved into cloud computing, this practice of creating a VLAN for each new customer has almost universally continued, with new virtual machines assigned to the VLAN's address space. Depending on the cloud infrastructure of the provider, this VLAN can be configured manually or automatically.

Continued use of VLANs within these environments makes sense, especially since many providers offer both hosting and cloud computing from the same facility; using a consistent VLAN approach allows for resource sharing and infrastructure simplicity.

This cloud computing utilization of VLANs has some drawbacks:

1. A delay in setting up of the account: Cloud computing services who have to manually build and configure VLANs place a delay in setting up the initial account. Some customers find the pause inconvenient; others see using that cloud computing provider as a barrier.

2. A restriction on the number of VLANs a router can manage: While this constraint can be overcome through the use of multiple routers, it adds difficulty to the network of the provider.

3. A limit on the number of computers that can be attached to a specific VLAN: Although many customers are unaffected, this limit is an unacceptable problem for web-scale applications that may require hundreds (if not thousands) of computers.

The Amazon alternative to VLANs Because Amazon wants to avoid the scaling constraints of VLAN technology in its cloud service, the VLAN approach is obviously unacceptable, for these reasons:

1. Limiting the number of VLANs would limit the number of customers Amazon could support with its AWS service. When Amazon first sketched out its plans for AWS, hundreds of thousands of different

customers were expected to use AWS eventually, so this limitation was too restrictive.

2. The limitation of a customer's number of computers within a single VLAN would limit the number of instances that might be used in its applications. Ama spanned hundreds, if not thousands, of cases, so it also wanted its customers to. A solution that restricts the number of computers each customer uses is clearly unacceptable.

Consequently, Amazon built the network very differently from traditional methods, and with these features, Amazon itself had experience with its application collection implementing a networking design: 3. Using Layer 3 technology across the infrastructure: all traffic is directly based on the IP address, with no reliance on MAC addressing from Layer 2.

4. The specifications that an IP address and all traffic to that instance be allocated to each instance must be driven by IP address: this is valid if traffic originates within AWS or externally — no exceptions.

5. No use or support of VLAN technology: Amazon has one or more IP address ranges within each area, and IP addresses are allocated randomly to customer instances within those address ranges. A corollary to this strategy is that all AWS IP addresses belong to Amazon, not to the client. So if a customer decides to move their website from their own data center to AWS, they will have a new IP address at the website.

AWS Direct Connect

The fact that all network traffic between AWS and non-AWS resources travels over the public Internet poses a major problem: although Internet connectivity is offered by very large service providers who have invested a great deal of money in their networks, the bandwidth and latency levels available to end-users are highly variable and may be unacceptable.

At the birth of the Internet, the seeds for these kinds of problems existed. By its very nature, the Internet is a shared network, where millions of packets of computers are intermingled as they are sent over the network. Packets from your machine jostle with those of everybody else. The upside is that a shared network is much simpler (say Hello to email and Facebook); the drawback is that there is much less reliable efficiency and throughput in a shared network.

It's not a big deal for you and me. If a Netflix video runs slowly, it's not an earth-shattering issue, and many of the things we do aren't greatly affected by network problems. E-mail, for example, usually works the same, with network throughput varying by as much as 1,000 per cent.

However, inconsistent network throughput can be a big issue for companies.

Okay, when you can't watch a video, you're going about your business and doing something else. However, if an employee is unable to watch a safety video, it can affect her ability to work, and paying someone who can not work is a big problem.

From the point of view of many businesses, another issue may occur: Internet traffic flows over a shared network and may require unauthorized access to data from a client. Sending traffic over a publicly accessible network is a no-no for certain businesses or certain types of data.

With Direct Connect, Amazon addresses the issue of traffic flowing through the public Internet: it allows a user to set up a private circuit between his data center and AWS to allow traffic to flow through a dedicated network connection without using the public Internet.

Direct Connect dedicated network connections, like Equinox, can be made from AWS to either a company's own data center or a public carrier. The company requesting the link to the Direct Connect network may have their servers located at the site of the public carrier or have a second connection to the company's own data center from the public carrier.

A dedicated network connection naturally addresses the issue of the protection of packets. A business using Direct Connect can be confident that its traffic on the network is free from prying eyes. In addition, to further ensure data security, it can enforce a virtual private network (VPN) between its AWS instances and its own data center. (Describing VPNs and how they work is beyond this book's scope, but it's enough to say they use clever software to encrypt data traveling across insecure networks— like the public Internet.) Amazon offers two levels of Direct Connect bandwidth: 1 Gbps and 10 Gbps.

For most connectivity needs, the former should be sufficient; the latter is sufficient for all but the most demanding high-performance computing and corresponds to the highest level of throughput within AWS itself.

Direct Connect comes with a financial arrangement similar to AWS: you only use Direct Connect when you need it, and you only pay for it when you use it.

For the 1 Gbps variant, Direct Connect costs $.30 per hour, and for the 10 Gbps variant $2.25 per hour. You don't pay for inbound network traffic as you might expect, and outbound traffic runs from $.03 to $.11 per gigabyte, depending on the region.

High-Performance AWS Networking

One concern about AWS networking is related to its performance — in my view, using the whole AWS infrastructure is the primary challenge. Amazon offers few specifics of its infrastructure, but I believe the company has 1 Gbps networking equipment in its data centers, which could provide technically acceptable performance for most applications, with 10 Gbps networking equipment used for more challenging AWS services, such as high-throughput instances. In other words, you're sharing the AWS network with some true hogs in the bandwidth, and the bandwidth competition can definitely affect the throughput of your application.

Most AWS users generally see approximately 100 Mbps throughput during their daily use of AWS in inter-instance network traffic. The problem is that although this average may be perfectly acceptable for many applications, the varying network load can alter that throughput significantly. Of course, 100 Mbps may be perfectly acceptable for some applications; however, 10 Mbps may even be too low for them. The problem is, you can't reliably predict your application's network throughput.

Many AWS users have vociferously complained about inconsistent AWS network performance and many AWS competitors have criticized the company, citing their own network design and capability as superior to AWS's and thus providing users with a reason for switching services.

To be sure, Amazon should upgrade the infrastructure to provide higher, more reliable network capacity. However, one drawback is that it would impose higher costs on all AWS users, including the masses of users who have no concerns about typical AWS networking performance.

Consequently, Amazon has developed an AWS-like solution, rather than reconstructing the networking infrastructure from the ground up: an additional set of offerings to address the needs of applications requiring high-performance networking. That solution leaves the vast majority of AWS users able to use the regular AWS service while at the same time providing another alternative for the smaller portion of users who need better networking.

The key phrase here, high-performance AWS networking, is focused on three types of unique instances: high I / O, compute cluster, and GPU clustering) This approach makes a lot of sense— after all, if you need a lot of network capacity, you're probably doing a lot of computing too. It's also sensible not to impose the higher cost of high-performance networking on users with more modest computing needs. This approach is consistent with Amazon's: Provide a cheap offer to those who don't need more than that, and extend the offer to those who want more and are willing to pay for it. This approach contrasts strongly with almost all other providers of cloud computing, which require all users to pay for expensive equipment, even if a user wants to run a small or non-mission-critical application only.

CHAPTER SIX: AMAZON WEB SERVICES

SECURITY

Countless polls have shown that security is the number one concern regarding cloud computing voiced by IT professionals. Deep down, many IT people distrust the security of cloud providers and believe they are the only ones that can really implement secure computing environments. And many types of IT are most skeptical regarding AWS security. Untold by many of them, but part of their visceral reactions to AWS, is, I think, a kind of disdain for the service, based on a prejudice that a "bookseller" may not be able to offer the same kind of computational security that "real" professionals provide.

Clouds Can Have Boundaries too. The key to understanding cloud security is the concept of confidence boundaries. The IT department takes responsibility for all protection throughout the system in on-site computing environments that you may be familiar with, no matter at what level or in which component a specific safety requirement exists. Conversely, in a public cloud setting. Only a portion of the overall security situation is applied and accepted by the supplier.

Here's a useful way to frame the discussion: a trust boundary concept sets a clear dividing line between the responsibilities of the service provider and your responsibilities. The provider manages security on one side of the trust boundary, and on the side of the trust boundary, you are responsible for the corresponding security.

This definition is not exclusive to AWS at all. For example, if your company uses Salesforce to handle customer interactions, Salesforce is responsible for the entire application for a significant amount of security. In fact, whenever you use the service of an external provider, you owe that provider some responsibility for protection. The obvious concern in these cases is how to share the burden with the provider.

So the key question about a cloud computing service is where does the trust boundary sit? Intuitively, in a Software as a Service (SaaS) offering like Salesforce, the trust boundary must be located on the spectrum at a spot where more of the security responsibility rests with the provider; after all, Salesforce not only runs the computing environment in which the application runs, but also develops, delivers, and assumes responsibility for the application itself.

Placing the trust boundary at the instance means that Amazon assumes responsibility for the security of these computer environment parts:

1. The physical facility: the data center; its people's access controls; and all electricity, cooling, and internet connectivity and networking from the perimeter of the building to the computer equipment

2. Computer hardware: all computers, storage and networking devices.

3. The hypervisor: the instance manager and the virtual machines in which instances run.

4. The underlying software infrastructure: the software that manages all AWS resources and offers the functionality that enables you to operate the application without communicating with another person

5. The Application programming order: Of course, as noted, security is a shared responsibility and there are some elements of security that remain with you.

6. Software packages for your application: they contain all the software that makes up your application, including any components of the software that you write.

7. Configuration of your application: To ensure the security of an application, configuring software packages correctly is often crucial to ensuring that no malevolent entity can access them and cause havoc.

The operating system of your application (possibly): This one is a bit tricky— and it's directly related to my earlier characterization of your security responsibility as "starting with the hypervisor" as "a bit glib." It all depends on who is responsible for the image you use. If you use an image created by someone else (either Amazon or a third party), the security for the operating system and the operating system bundles lies with the image supplier, including not only the general operating system (e.g. Windows 2008 or Ubuntu Linux) but also all the patches to the operating system, system software (e.g. identity management system) and, probably, midway through.

The Deperimeterization of Security

If assessing the different security obligations, you may need to consider the effects of a concept known as security deperimeterisation.

(Of course, you might have to ask yourself how you're supposed to consider a word you can't even pronounce?) Let me give you a little background: the idea of deperimeterisation comes from the work done by the Jericho Forum, an industry research organization that is part of The Open Organization. The core conviction of its founders is that traditional computing security measures, which are focused on stopping threats at the perimeter of the data center, are insufficient in today's computing environments.

With the rise of repeated attacks by criminal and state actors, the covert installation and ongoing monitoring by advanced persistent threats (APT), and the constantly evolving viruses and malware that present zero-day dangers (dangers that require immediate responses instead of letting you wait for updates to virus scan databases or malware detection services), you can no longer assume that security measures on the outside of your computing resources are sufficient.

The Jericho Forum recommends that everyone recognize the successful security deperimeterisation and thus acknowledge that:

1. There must be security measures on every computing tool.

2. Such interventions must be capable of protecting the property without relying on security services dependent on external perimeters. Amazon doesn't require you to mount an IDS / IPS system on its network, because

3. It would find that behavior to be unacceptable for its operation and for the regulation it requires in order to properly run AWS.

4. More importantly, other AWS customers would consider your safety device a security threat to their applications. Any surveillance system that tracks traffic would be regarded as an invasive device by other users who tries to inspect their traffic, which they would find unacceptable.

Installing host-based intrusion detection software, or HIDS, on your AWS instances is the way to address the problem. (The IDS letters also include IPS— even techie types could not tolerate a HIDS / HIPS acronym.) HIDS performs almost the same task as an IDS / IPS appliance but does not allow any equipment to be mounted on the network.

How does deperimeterisation impact the critical boundary of trust between your area of responsibility and the area of Amazon? Not that, to be honest.

The definition of deperimeterisation provides the context for what is happening but does not really alter the fundamental nature of your relationship with Amazon, since

1. Amazon continues to be responsible for all computer environment security, up to and including the hypervisor. Actually, as I said earlier, this is not entirely accurate because Amazon is responsible for the virtual machine's creation and operation. Additionally, Amazon is also responsible for the security of the image if you are using an AWS file.

It must ensure that the appropriate operating system update, all required updates and suitable modifications are implemented. Amazon manages and configures all hardware and software, and you don't have to do anything about AWS security (and actually can't do anything).

2. You are still responsible for the security and overall application of the running case. This involves all the software that runs in the case, whether it was developed by you (or your organization) or from a third-party supplier (commercial or open-source community).

You control and customize the whole program, and Amazon has nothing to do with that. (Indeed, it shouldn't do anything, because accessing your resources would be a major betrayal of confidence and a valid reason for customers to abandon the service.) However, in one place, you and Amazon share some responsibility for security: at the interface between Amazon's area of responsibility and yours. Logically enough, that interface is the network interface— where network traffic leaves Amazon's environment and gets into your case.

Aws Security Groups

Each instance includes an AWS virtual network interface, and Amazon implements a software firewall on each instance. The firewall is there for traffic management to and from the case.

Each instance launches a firewall which is clamped shut by default—no traffic can enter the instance. As you might imagine, this often makes it useless, unless it does computing activities which are self-contained.

Consequently, you must actively allow access to your instance through the network.

(If you've ever had the misfortune of running a Linux machine device firewall, take heart: Amazon makes the job much simpler by using protection groups.)

The following elements of network traffic access are regulated by safety community rules:

1. Traffic protocol: Security groups accept and refer to three types of network traffic:

• Transmission Control Protocol (TCP)

• User Datagram Program (UDP): This less complex network protocol than TCP is hardly used, so you can safely ignore it.

• Internet Control Message Protocol (ICMP): This protocol is used to support some network monitoring commands and to send error messages for applications.

2. Traffic source: The aim is to monitor the sources from which a security group receives traffic. (My guess is that you probably won't use this protocol much, either.) The security group can be set to allow traffic from everyone, from just one particular IP address, from a range of IP addresses, or from other security group members.

3. Traffic port: TCP traffic passes between ports which can be viewed as individual network connections within the overall connectivity of the network.

Usually, ports are connected with specific applications, and all traffic to a particular port is directed towards that application. Port 80, for example, is used to support web traffic (or, more specifically, HTTP traffic).

One wants to confine the traffic of a port to a single application; otherwise, when two applications try to read network traffic on a single port, you run into problems— where should the packet be sent?

Security Groups

Each account has one security group pre-defined: default. Default begins with no traffic being permitted to enter the instance, so no traffic can hit the instance every time you start an instance with the initial default security group governing which network traffic is approved.

You can also create additional security groups and put rules inside the new security groups. An AWS account can have up to 500 security groups per security group and 100 laws.

Security group rules To allow traffic into an instance, open one or more ports by establishing a default security group rule. For instance, you can create a rule to allow the input of HTTP traffic into the instance.

Clearly, the law can be applied using the AWS API. Most people, however, use the AWS Management Console to determine guidelines.

Security Group Best Practices

As it serves a vital function, the security group is a critical feature: it manages traffic in your instances. Understanding and implementing security groups is important to ensure the proper and safe operation of your applications. Follow this compilation of best security group practices:

1. Evict the use of the security group Default. Although the Default Security Group can open ports, avoid doing so— create separate security groups for all network traffic laws, instead. It is a lazy tactic to use default settings and contributes to poorly thought-out architecture and practices.

2. Use famous names. When you use names that provide helpful information, it's much easier to decide which security group to apply to which case. This may not seem difficult, but believe me— you will appreciate any help you can get when you start managing over 100 different security groups.

3. Just open the ports that you need to access. Cloud computing has nothing to do with this time-honored suggestion. Reducing the number

of open ports reduces the chances of attacking malevolent agents, so open ports only for the facilities or applications you need.

4. Applications regarding partitioning. Use security groups to partition applications is a good practice for scope implementation of protection and that the potential for malevolent actors to have access to important application resources. Make sure you build versions of security groups to support the various versions of the application that you'll end up running 5. Restrict access to administrator system. You can limit system administrator access to your instances, by using CIDR masks, to computers located in locations you trust, such as your corporate offices. When workers work from home or on the path, you can set up a Virtual Private Network (VPN) from their machines to the corporate network and then forward traffic to the AWS system administrator via the corporate network, where it conforms to the CIDR masking that you have   introduced.

CHAPTER SEVEN: ADDITIONAL CORE

SERVICES OF AWS

AWS has its core services— such as S3, EC2, Amazon Glacier, and Amazon EBS — but this isn't the end of the story. Amazon operates according to the principle of "variety is the spice of life," so as well as the big players, it offers quite a range of services. The idea is to help you understand the breadth of Amazon's products and give you the confidence that you will at least be familiar with every product in the industry's most comprehensive cloud service offering.

Understanding the Other Services of AWS

AWS is At the center of the AWS universe are certain foundational services — EC2, S3, Amazon EBS and Amazon Glacier —. For two reasons, I refer to them as basic:

1. They include the first market-introduced AWS services.

AWS started out with S3 and followed up with EC2 within the year. AWS networking and security were critical components of the operation of the entire AWS environment and components of S3 and EC2. Many storage options that I cover were not part of early AWS services but included with S3 for compatibility purposes.

2. These services are the basis of how you use the AWS. Although other AWS services can definitely be leveraged without the use of storage

and computing, the vast majority of people use those services in combination with storage and computing. The "additional" programs complement and increasing the utility of the core services.

They help you build better applications using the simple storage and computing resources AWS provides. For instance, Elastic Load Balancer (ELB) is an additional service that Amazon provides to disperse traffic to multiple web servers, enabling the application to accept more traffic than a single web server can handle. To deploy a simple AWS application, you do not need an ELB, but the software makes running a high-traffic, AWS-based web application much simpler.

If you were to use a "traditional" PaaS system, it would automatically have load balancing — you probably wouldn't even be aware of it being in operation, but the company would arrange for enough web server resources to support traffic in your application and set up a load balancing process to disperse traffic between those web servers.

That's all fine and dandy except there's a lot of traffic management options.

Sometimes it's round-robin (every server gets traffic in turn), sometimes it's based on the server's processor load (lightly loaded servers get more traffic), and sometimes it's based on which server has the least number of active links. In a conventional PaaS program, you're stuck with whatever delivery tool the service provides and you're out of luck if it doesn't fit the needs of your application.

So Amazon, in its quest to provide its customers with more options, provides ELB, which offers a great deal of versatility, is easy to use, and is affordable.

However, if it does not meet the requirements of your application, this is no problem— you are free to implement your own solution (or take advantage of one of the many open-source or commercial solutions that other organizations make available within AWS).

The key difference between the product offerings of Amazon and what you can expect from the conventional offerings of the Product as a Service (Paas) is that Amazon provides a service designed to help you build and run your program, but does not require you to use it. You are free to address the load-balancing needs of your application in a different way, if you wish. And that's true of all AWS services— they provide services that are commonly needed, but you're the driver's seat. Feel free or not to use them.

This solution seems to be the best one for these kinds of services— instead of providing a series of handcuffs that limit how you meet your needs, AWS provides a stepladder to make it easier for you to reach your goals.

Aside from hokey images, the bottom line is this: AWS has a number of services that you can leverage to help build your application, but you have complete control and choice about them— if they're helpful, it's great, but if you want to do something else, it's okay. Amazon doesn't control how you have to achieve your goals.

Deciding Whether It Makes Sense to Use Other AWs

It's time for brass tacks: What are the benefits you can realize by using what Amazon offers instead of implementing the functionality of your own application?

Alternatively, what are the reasons you would not be using these services for?

It may help to list all of the pros and cons. First, here are some important reasons you'd be using core AWS and extended services— because they can

1. Offer needed features outside of your area of expertise: Extension services offer something you need for your application in an area you don't know much about — and have no time to learn.

You might need load balancing, for example, but have never implemented it. (And trust me, properly running load balancing is an ancient art; one application performance expert told me that the number one performance bottleneck he sees is misconfigured load balancers.) Instead of devoting time to learning about load balancing, using Amazon's service— you know it has world-class experts working on its Elastic Load Balancer.

2. Simplify application development: Using Amazon's service makes the application easier to create. Taking advantage of AWS core and expanded resources makes the entire application easier to build.

3. Improve the time to market: Using AWS infrastructure means less work for you so you can launch your application faster. There is always time pressure on the delivery of software and the use of AWS services helps you to deliver your applications faster. In a way, it's an extension of the general argument for using AWS — just as the AWS foundation services accelerate the provision of basic computing functionality, the additional core and expanded services accelerate the development of application capability.

4. Achieve scalability: Managing scalability is challenging, and managing high load volatility can be even more difficult, which requires constant capacity growth and reduction. Not only does Amazon make buying as much of a service as you need simple, it also manages all the plumbing information for you.

5. Integrates with other AWS services that you are using: If you write an application in AWS, you can be sure that both core and extended AWS services work well not only with AWS storage and EC2 computing but also with each other. A definite advantage of using AWS services is not having to jury-rigge different applications to get them to work with each other.

6. Save you money: AWS only provides the services it can deliver via automation, so no (costly) manual interaction is required from Amazon staff. The company is constantly focusing on cutting costs.

The AWS service will therefore probably be less expensive than if you were to implement it yourself.

Allow you to focus on differentiated application functionality: Most additional AWS services fall into the category of functionality required but unexciting. Or put it another way, AWS resources include plumbing your application— it's important but nothing that consumers of your application would ever see as something special relevant to your application. These programs are undifferentiating in Silicon Valley-speak— they do nothing to make the application stand apart from any other program. To extend this example, no application user ever said, "Boy, the reason I like this application is because it does a terrific load balancing job!"If you use AWS services to provide undifferentiated functionality, you will have more time to focus on functionality that makes your application different from others. This benefit is perhaps the most important of the additional AWS services— they allow you to focus on your application's most important aspects.

Working with (Identity And Access Management) IAM

It's been claimed for a long time that AWS's strength is that it makes it easy to get the tools to build and deploy applications. Nevertheless, the blessing of simplicity often carries with it a bit of curse— potentially, at least. It turns out that when AWS was first introduced, one way that AWS made its "easy" use was in account handling and user management: there was to be one (and only one) user for each account, and it was presumed that the account and all the resources associated with the account were "managed." Although this arrangement seems reasonable, it represents a significant shortcoming for many businesses using AWS, particularly those referred to as enterprises in the technology industry.

Companies typically have multiple organizations involved in the application lifecycle— development, for one; operations, quality assurance, and testing, for another. Multiple individuals can carry out administrative functions on the application within each of these organizations. Once AWS was initially launched, it meant that the program and the AWS services it ran in could be managed by between 10 and 40 people, but all had to share a single identity.

In addition, most organizations would use a single private key to control administrative access to AWS instances and built-in software components. It would then have to share this single, private key among all users.

Beginning to see the problem? You have a scenario where perhaps 40 people share the identity of a single user and that identity just happens to give the user full control of all AWS resources. In other words, there's no way for you to restrict access to only such services for a specific user.

In many IT departments, alarm bells that ring out because they may be perfectly willing to provide developers with complete administrative access to development instances, but they will want to prohibit developers from administrative access to instances that are part of a production deployment.

With corporations, an even bigger problem is what to do when someone leaves the company. A former employee simply should not be able to access services, but denying access to him would require all remaining employees to reissue new credentials and keys. In an IT company with dozens or hundreds (or thousands!) of workers, it would be a nightmare to have to reissue credentials any time a person leaves... As you can see, the "easy" way of doing things — going with a single user identity and credential setting— has brought complications in a boatload.

Fortunately for us, to address these complexities, Amazon has created its Identity and Access Management (IAM) service, a way to tweak access control and the AWS credential environment in ways that make the system more enterprise user-friendly. IAM is automatically included with every AWS account and there's nothing you need to do to enable it.

What is even worse, all existing resources (e.g. running instances) would have to be terminated and relaunched with new credentials, which would impact the uptime of applications.

IAM Functionality

IAM provides some great features:

1. User management: You can create multiple accounts in a single account and provide different account access controls for the resources. Users can also be assigned to groups, and group-level access controls can

be assigned, which will then implement those controls for each person within the group.

2. Centralized control of user identities and access credentials: IAM is used to manage all user identities and credentials, thereby centralizing and simplifying a complex and important mechanism for control.

3. AWS resource controls: By putting restrictions on different AWS resources, you can control what users can access, provided the AWS resources. For example, you may allow certain users within your organization to access company data stored in S3 while preventing other users who do not need access to the data from interacting with the S3 object.

4. AWS manages resource creation: You can limit where users can build AWS resources. For example, if you want to ensure that new instances are only launched by users in the US West region, IAM can be used to enforce that rule.

5. AWS sharing of resources across accounts: You can give people in other accounts access to AWS services inside your account. This can be helpful if you want your organization to collaborate with a partner company, or if your company uses specific department accounts.

6. Consolidated billing: For all user activity within AWS, you will receive a single bill instead of a separate bill for each account. Billing consolidation simplifies the expense control, as it allows for quick

analysis of all AWS expenses in a single billing statement. It also decreases your total AWS bill, as you can take advantage of reduced prices associated with higher rates of AWS resource use and make better use of booking prices

Integrating Supplementary AWS Services into Your Application

Amazon's approach to application services has one major advantage: it provides them on a use-if-you-choose basis. Nothing prevents you from using another product or service to implement the same functionality as one of the services offered by Amazon — even if you decide to run that product or service in AWS.

In your application, two tasks are present when using a core AWS services:

1. Create and configure your own service.

2. Use the service in your case.

As for the first mission, using the Amazon alternative for a given service is usually much easier compared to setting up your own. For example, filling out a brief wizard to create, say, a large memcached pool and letting Amazon take care of creating the instances, installing the memcached software, configuring them to talk to each other, and managing their uptime, for example, is far easier than performing all those tasks yourself.

I don't even mention the fact that (okay, I am) your interest is in the functionality of the service, not the management of the service per se. In other words, if you do it yourself, you have to do all of the work yourself to gain the benefits of the core service. By contrast, you gain the benefits of the service using the Amazon variant without having to invest any of your precious time in administering it.

Based on your estimation of your time, you should make an assessment of the financial benefits of having Amazon to assume responsibility relative to the cost of the Amazon service. I think in most situations, financially speaking, you'd be better off using the Amazon service.

Concerning the second task— using the service from within the application — Amazon's approach to providing these services shows its knowledge.

Instead of creating a different or comprehensive solution requiring you to develop an offer-specific usage model, Amazon has typically left the usage model unchanged, or close to the model used by the alternatives you would use if you decided to implement the feature yourself. For example, while Amazon's RDS service offers real benefits in terms of database administration activities, it does not force any change on you to communicate with the RDS-managed databases.

It is fair to say that the differences between the established products which Amazon mirrors in order to create its core services and the Amazon variant are small enough that it is not particularly difficult to use the core service and does not impose a difficult learning curve.

That approach to these services, which fall under the umbrella of the Platform-as-a-Service (PaaS), is quite different from the other. Different functionality is available in those offerings, but it is so closely associated with the PaaS service that using it involves learning a new methodology and sometimes a completely different process to obtain the same result as with existing goods.

I am a strong proponent of the Amazon approach, as you can probably tell because I feel it offers the greatest productivity and financial benefits while imposing the smallest disruption in application design and implementation or skill-building.

Choosing an AWS System Compatibility Strategy

It's important to take the right approach to select key AWS resources to leverage. Such programs are huge productivity boosters, but it doesn't make sense to needlessly incorporate them into your program. Here are the recommended guidelines:

1. If you have no expertise in this service area, then rely on the AWS experts to run it. We are all pressed for time and it is wasteful and futile to learn a new skill while under the fire. You're unlikely to be better at it

than Amazon is and you can more productively spend your resources in places where you have the experience.

2. If this field of operation does not provide specific features or distinguish the query, depend on the AWS service. While your application may be much more convenient for your users if you have its content stored locally, no one will purchase your service because you have personally deployed a collection of geographically distributed servers to enable low-latency access. Focusing on what's in the content, not on how the content is delivered, will serve you better. Rely on CloudFront for what it's good at, and channel your resources to something that delivers consumer value.

If this service is one you're not sure you can provide far less expensively than Amazon does, then rely on Amazon to introduce it. Most IT departments are bad at calculating their true costs of providing a service, so if there's even a possibility Amazon could be more cost-effective, you're better served by using AWS, because Amazon actually runs it far less expensively than you can.

CHAPTER EIGHT: MANAGING THE

EXPENSES OF AWS

This chapter discusses two significant and interrelated concerns for users of AWS:

• How to ensure the efficient and effective operation of your AWS systems

• How to better handle your AWS costs

Amazon is known for its ability to run AWS on a scale, its successful use of technology and its track record of maintaining extra low costs. However, the ability of Amazon to run AWS efficiently and cost-effectively doesn't automatically mean that the resources you run in AWS are efficient and cheap.

AWS Costs — Complicated Amazon is completely transparent about charging for its services, unlike many of its competitors posting such statements on their websites: "For pricing, please contact a sales representative to review your requirements." (You will never find out what those providers charge unless you are subject to a sales pitch). Moreover, Amazon is to be lauded for its creativity in rolling out new services.

It rolled out two new major services and a plethora of small improvements to its existing services just during the writing of this book. Furthermore, the company should be commended for developing its EC2 reserved instances offering which reduces total ownership costs (TCO). And Amazon, of course, deserves credit for providing price breaks for bulk use.

The difficulty of monitoring Amazon costs stems from all that praiseworthy and praiseworthy conduct. Simply put, Amazon has quickly introduced such a variety of services and pricing structures that attempting to grasp all the costs that are charged to your account is quite a challenge; it's even worse when you have complicated applications that use a lot of different AWS resources spread over multiple levels— not to mention trying to understand how different application loads (which typically cause loading) are.

Throughout its brief lifespan, AWS has grown from a limited set of services provided with a limited set of options to a diverse mix of services and options that are much harder to track and that function toward TCO's simple prediction.

Obviously, you should fully understand your resource utilization, figure out its patterns, and analyze what you can do to ensure that the cost of your AWS is as low as possible; on the other hand, you don't want to reduce your costs to the point where the availability or performance of your application suffers.

Managing Your AWS Costs Now that you know that AWS is a big deal, that you're likely to use a lot of it, and that managing it in a cost-effective manner is challenging, you probably want guidelines to make sure you get your money's worth out of AWS.

You have come to the right place, as there are some suggestions for best practice here:

1. Applications design to be scalable— both up and down. Using multiple smaller instances of EC2 instead of a smaller number of bigger ones. It means that you suit the overall processing power to the application load more closely so that at any given time you have exactly the right amount available.

2. Follow a strategy for managing applications "down and out." This concept, coined by Forrester analyst James Staten, means that when the application load shrinks you should try to have only the right amount of computing resources available at any given point, and that you should actively reduce computing resources. The easy, immediate AWS provisioning capability supports this because you can easily add resources to your application if the application load increases. And if you followed the previous advice on making your application scalable, your application would easily accommodate a resource pool that is increasing or diminishing.

3. Leverage category Auto Scaling. Operations burden is one challenge to adopt the "down and off" strategy (and the "up and on" complement to respond to increasing application load). An operator has

to do some work for every instance that needs to be started or terminated: adding or subtracting the instance to a resource pool, linking it to other instances, and maybe adding a load balancer to the mix. Using Auto Scaling groups to deal with this pressure, the AWS addresses this question. Configure your application upfront, then let Amazon take care of scaling your resource pool dynamically while you sit back with a cup of coffee.

4. Use an Amazon or a third-party AWS management tool.

Auto Scaling groups are awesome to handle EC2, but as the survey data indicates, you'll be using plenty of other AWS tools. AWS management tools may reduce the overhead for handling those other services, including SQS and RDS.

5. Perform application load testing to help with your financial modeling. (That's less work and more coffee break time!)

You can see what resources it uses at higher volumes by loading up your application with simulated traffic. You can then see if you are likely to expand your use of those facilities enough to obtain volume-based price breaks. Conversely, it also demonstrates if you use other services wastefully at greater workload loads and can restructure your application to reduce the use of those services and save money. Naturally, I advocate load testing to ensure better robustness of the application; it is an additional benefit of load testing and performance testing.

A number of products and services providing open-source and commercial load / performance testing are available. One I like is from SOASTA (www.soasta.com), a CloudTest service provider.

Of course, it's a cloud-based on-demand service that allows you to use (and pay) only for what you need. SOASTA also provides the free CloudTest Lite app that can be mounted on your local machine, allowing you to test up to 100 simultaneous users. Frankly, you'd be foolish not to use CloudTest Lite, considering that it's free, and how necessary it is to develop and test an application to be stable in the face of large and fluctuating prices.

6. Use software for the review to ensure the efficient and effective use of AWS. As you can see from the results of the survey at the beginning of this chapter, the use of AWS is simple. In reality, it's so simple you can easily lose track of what you're using — or, to be more accurate, what you're providing, and paying for, but not using. Believe me: It is easy to forget all the services that you have supplied. This is not a sign of oblivion or carelessness; it just happens. What's important is what you should do to fix this simple provisioning byproduct of AWS.

Use the Cloudyn analytics platform (www.cloudyn.com). Other third-party analytics tools are on the marketplace and Amazon recently launched the new Trusted Advisor service, which is free to use and performs some of the same analytical types. In addition, most third-party providers offer a free-use tier. Given the actual cost of unused AWS services and the availability of free-use levels of software such as Trusted

Advisor and other third-party applications, you should at least use an analysis tool to provide you with a reading of where you stand with the use of AWS. If the findings indicate any flaws in your usage patterns (and they'll probably — trust me), you should look at doing a more thorough analysis by switching from third-party tools like Cloudyn to one of the paid choices.

THANKS FOR TAKING TIME TO READ THIS BOOK, YOU HAVE LEARNED AND ITS BEST TO PRACTICE WHAT YOU LEARNT ABOUT AMAZON WEB SERVICES.

NOW GO AND EXPLORE!!!